But my Totem saw the shame;
from his ridgepole shrine he came,
And he told me in a vision of the night: —
'There are nine and sixty ways
of constructing tribal lays,
And every single one of them is right!'

—Rudyard Kipling, *In the Neolithic Age*

O God, I could be bounded in
a nutshell and count myself a king
of infinite space...

—Shakespeare, *Hamlet*

7-DAY USE
RETURN TO DESK FROM WHICH BORROWED
THANK YOU

TITLE:	ONE WEEK IN THE LIBRARY
AUTHOR:	W. Maxwell Prince

DUE DATE	BORROWER'S NAME
ARTIST	John Amor
COLORIST	Kathryn Layno
LETTERS	Good Old Neon
COVER ART	Frazer Irving
CHARTS	Ashley Walker
COVER DESIGN	Tom Muller

978-1534300224
(1534300228)
96 p

GENERAL INQUIRIES
wmaxwellprince@gmail.com
BROOKLYN

ONE WEEK IN THE LIBRARY. First printing. December 2016. Published by Image Comics, Inc. Office of publication: 2001 Center Street, Sixth Floor, Berkeley, CA 94704. Copyright © 2016 W. Maxwell Prince. All rights reserved. "One Week in the Library," its logos, and the likenesses of all characters herein are trademarks of W. Maxwell Prince, unless otherwise noted. "Image" and the Image Comics logos are registered trademarks of Image Comics, Inc. No part of this publication may be reproduced or transmitted, in any form or by any means (except for short excerpts for journalistic or review purposes), without the express written permission of W. Maxwell Prince or Image Comics, Inc. All names, characters, events, and locales in this publication are entirely fictional. Any resemblance to actual persons (living or dead), events, or places, without satiric intent, is coincidental. Printed in the USA. For information regarding the CPSIA on this printed material call: 203-595-3636 and provide reference #RICH–714937. For international rights, contact: foreignlicensing@imagecomics.com. ISBN 978-1-5343-0022-4. Book design by Good Old Neon.

ONE
WEEK
IN THE
LIBRARY

IMAGE COMICS, INC.
Robert Kirkman – Chief Operating Officer; Erik Larsen – Chief Financial Officer
Todd McFarlane – President; Marc Silvestri – Chief Executive Officer
Jim Valentino – Vice-President; Eric Stephenson – Publisher
Corey Murphy – Director of Sales; Jeremy Sullivan – Director of Digital Sales
Jeff Boison – Director of Publishing Planning & Book Trade Sales
Kat Salazar – Director of PR & Marketing; Branwyn Bigglestone – Controller
Drew Gill – Art Director; Jonathan Chan – Production Manager
Meredith Wallace – Print Manager; Briah Skelly – Publicist
Sasha Head – Sales & Marketing Production Designer
Randy Okamura – Digital Production Designer
David Brothers – Branding Manager
Olivia Ngai – Content Manager
Addison Duke – Production Artist
Vincent Kukua – Production Artist
Tricia Ramos – Production Artist
Jeff Stang – Direct Market Sales Representative
Emilio Bautista – Digital Sales Associate
Leanna Caunter – Accounting Assistant
Chloe Ramos-Peterson – Library Market Sales Representative
IMAGECOMICS.COM

THURSDAY

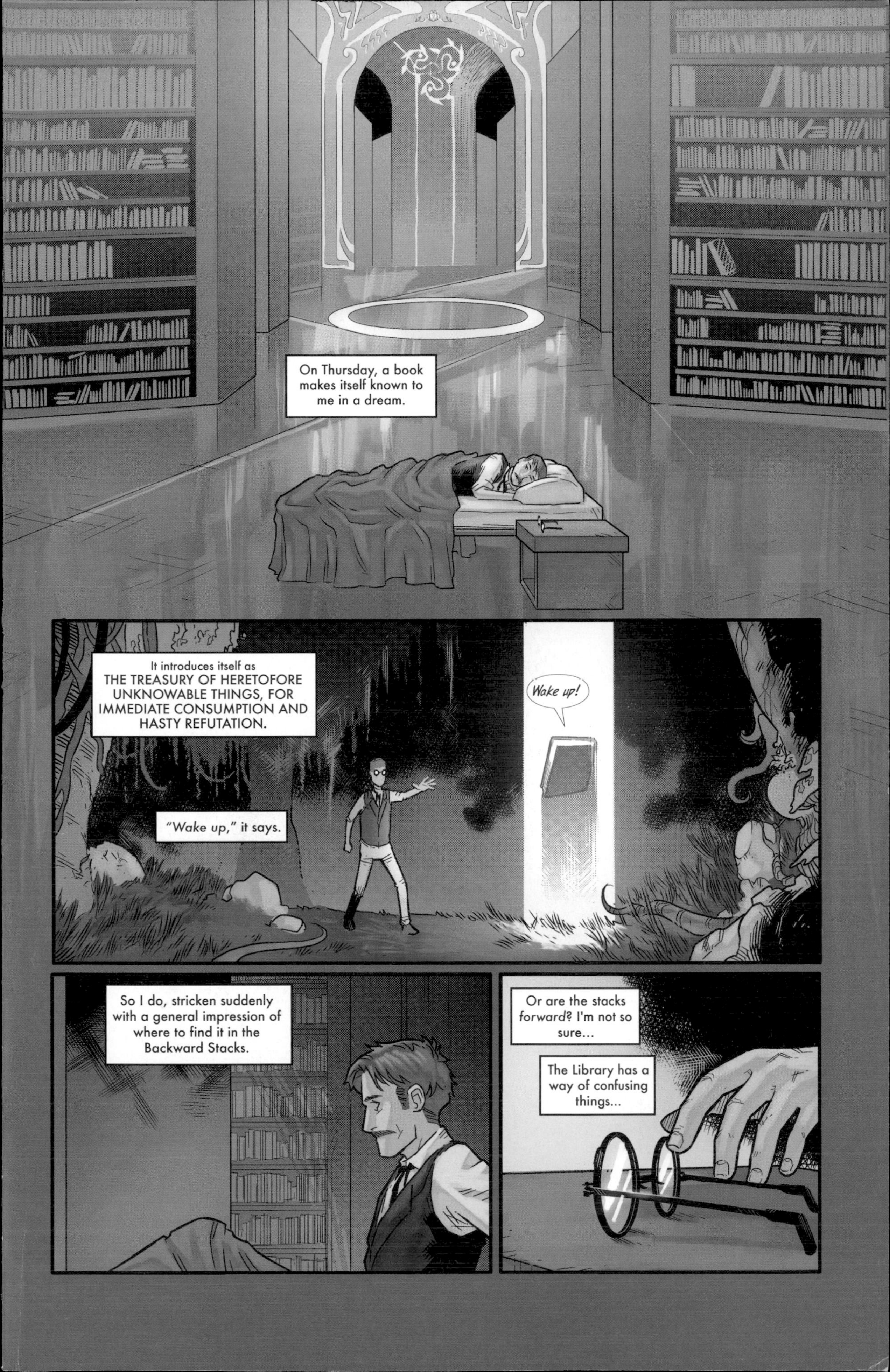
On Thursday, a book makes itself known to me in a dream.
It introduces itself as THE TREASURY OF HERETOFORE UNKNOWABLE THINGS, FOR IMMEDIATE CONSUMPTION AND HASTY REFUTATION.
Wake up!
"Wake up," it says.
So I do, stricken suddenly with a general impression of where to find it in the Backward Stacks.
Or are the stacks forward? I'm not so sure...
The Library has a way of confusing things...

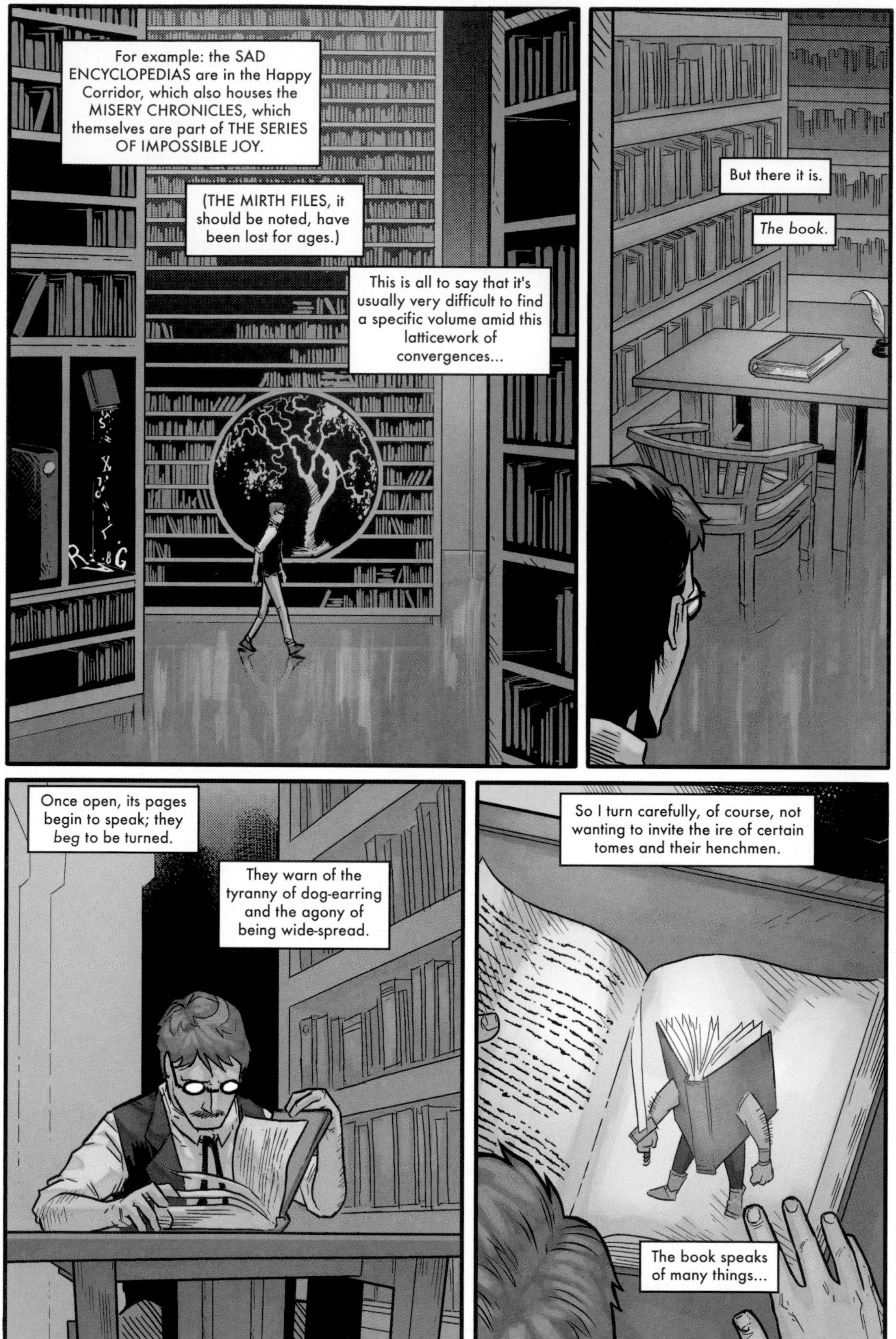
For example: the SAD ENCYCLOPEDIAS are in the Happy Corridor, which also houses the MISERY CHRONICLES, which themselves are part of THE SERIES OF IMPOSSIBLE JOY.
(THE MIRTH FILES, it should be noted, have been lost for ages.)
This is all to say that it's usually very difficult to find a specific volume amid this latticework of convergences...
But there it is.
The book.
Once open, its pages begin to speak; they *beg* to be turned.
They warn of the tyranny of dog-earring and the agony of being wide-spread.
So I turn carefully, of course, not wanting to invite the ire of certain tomes and their henchmen.
The book speaks of many things...

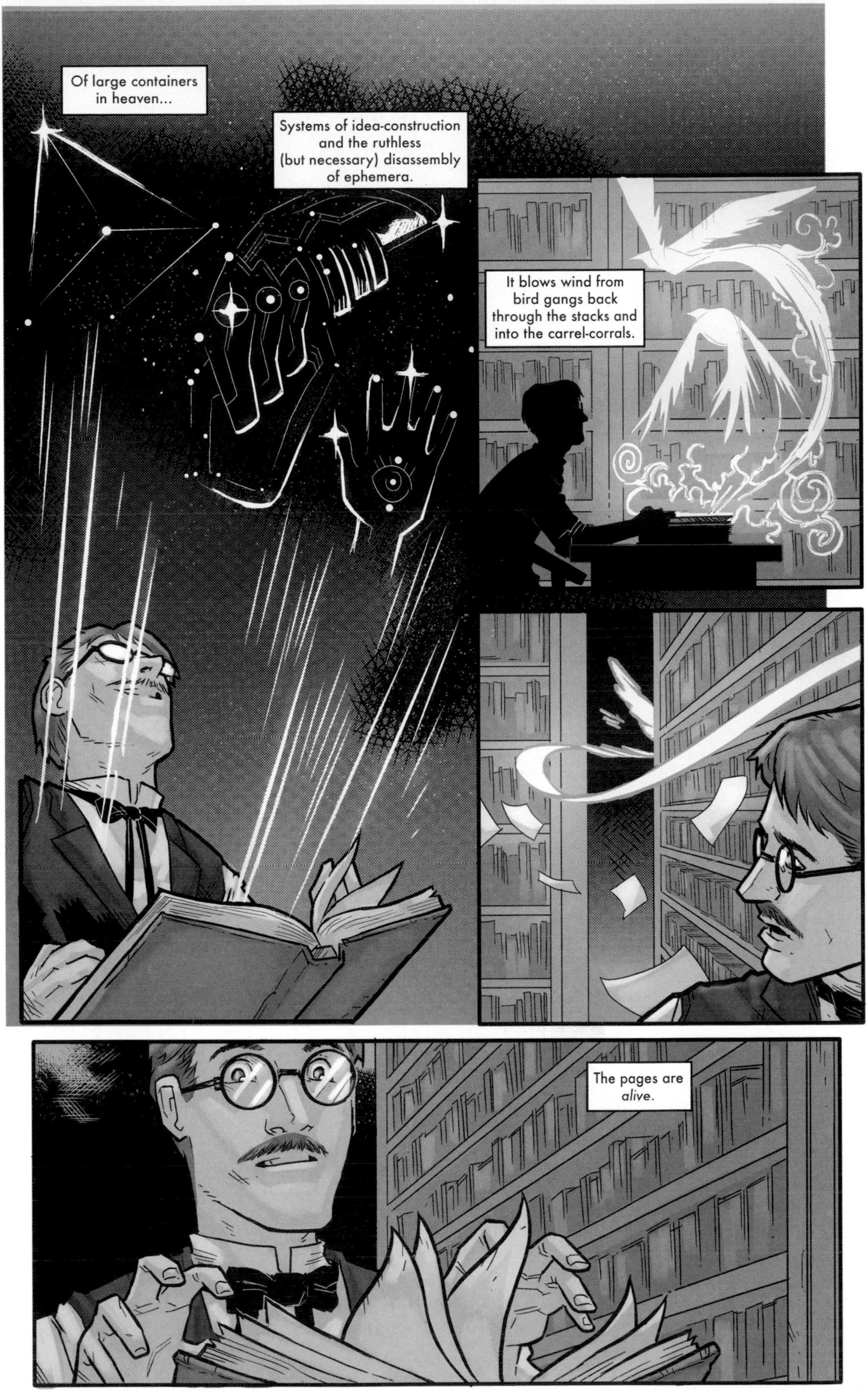
Of large containers in heaven...
Systems of idea-construction and the ruthless (but necessary) disassembly of ephemera.
It blows wind from bird gangs back through the stacks and into the carrel-corrals.
The pages are *alive*.

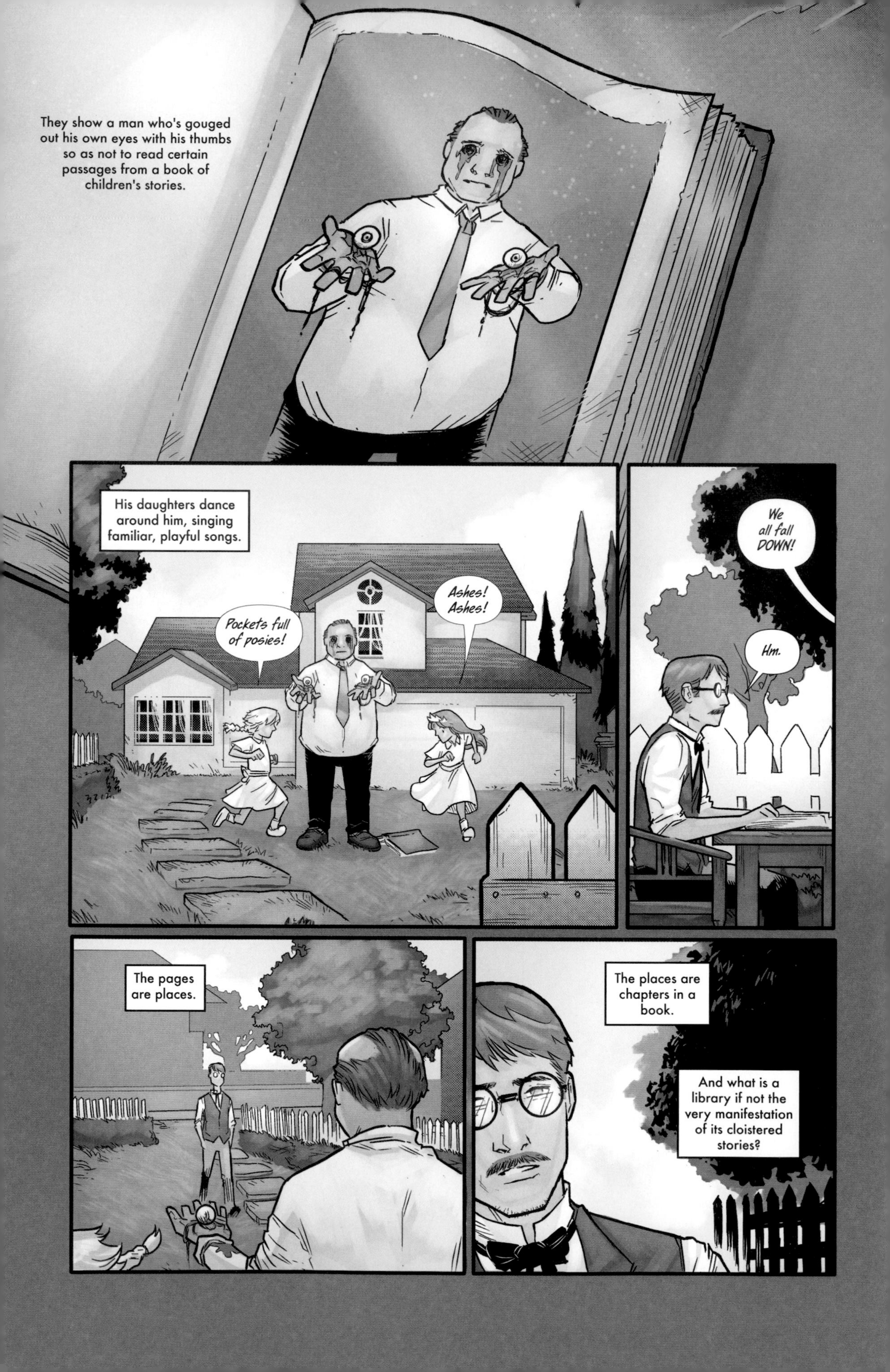
They show a man who's gouged out his own eyes with his thumbs so as not to read certain passages from a book of children's stories.
His daughters dance around him, singing familiar, playful songs.
Pockets full of posies!
Ashes! Ashes!
We all fall DOWN!
Hm.
The pages are places.
The places are chapters in a book.
And what is a library if not the very manifestation of its cloistered stories?

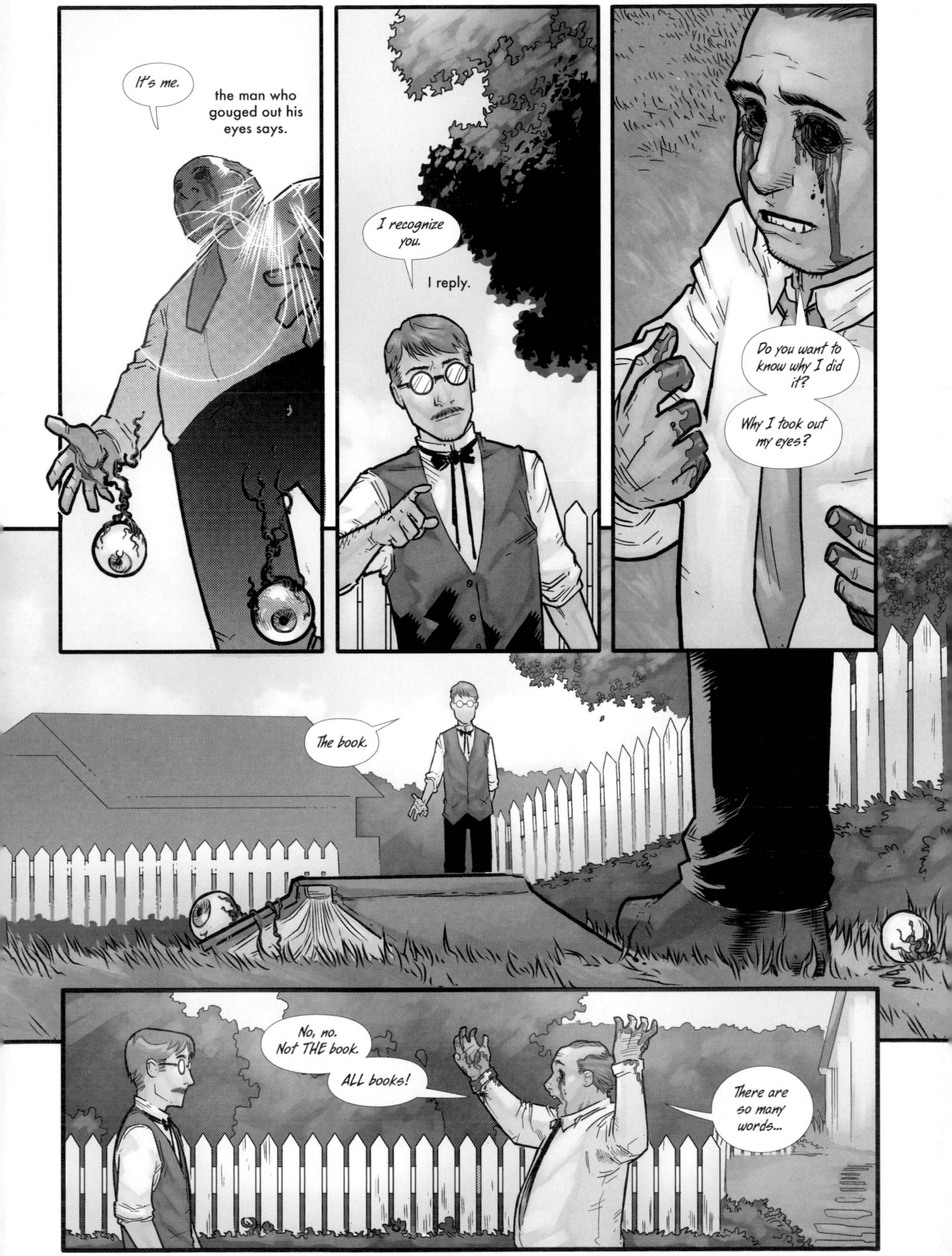
It's me.
the man who gouged out his eyes says.
I recognize you.
I reply.
Do you want to know why I did it?
Why I took out my eyes?
The book.
No, no. Not THE book.
ALL books!
There are so many words...

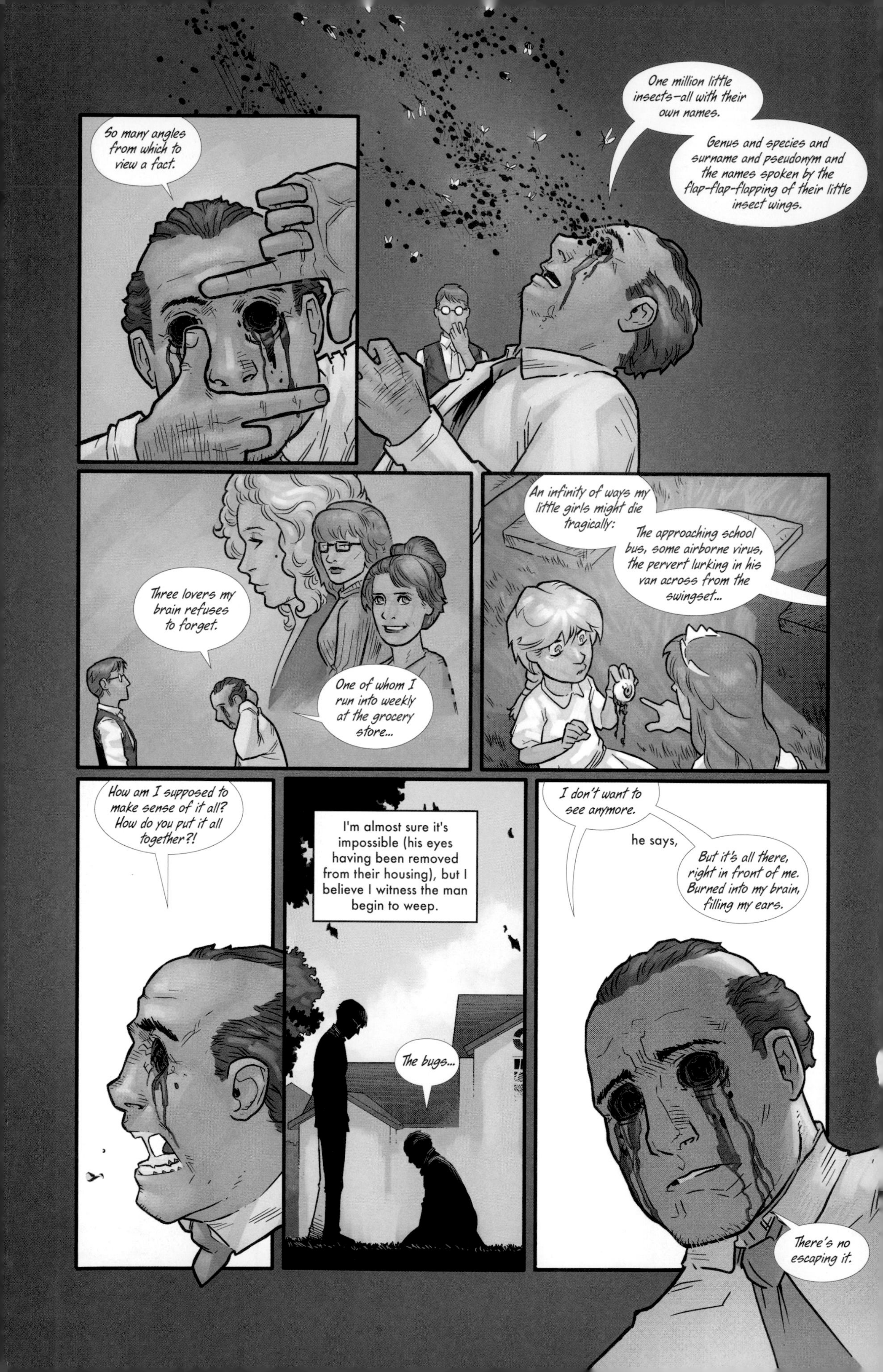
So many angles from which to view a fact.
One million little insects—all with their own names.
Genus and species and surname and pseudonym and the names spoken by the flap-flap-flapping of their little insect wings.
Three lovers my brain refuses to forget.
One of whom I run into weekly at the grocery store...
An infinity of ways my little girls might die tragically:
The approaching school bus, some airborne virus, the pervert lurking in his van across from the swingset...
How am I supposed to make sense of it all? How do you put it all together?!
I'm almost sure it's impossible (his eyes having been removed from their housing), but I believe I witness the man begin to weep.
The bugs...
I don't want to see anymore.
he says,
But it's all there, right in front of me. Burned into my brain, filling my ears.
There's no escaping it.

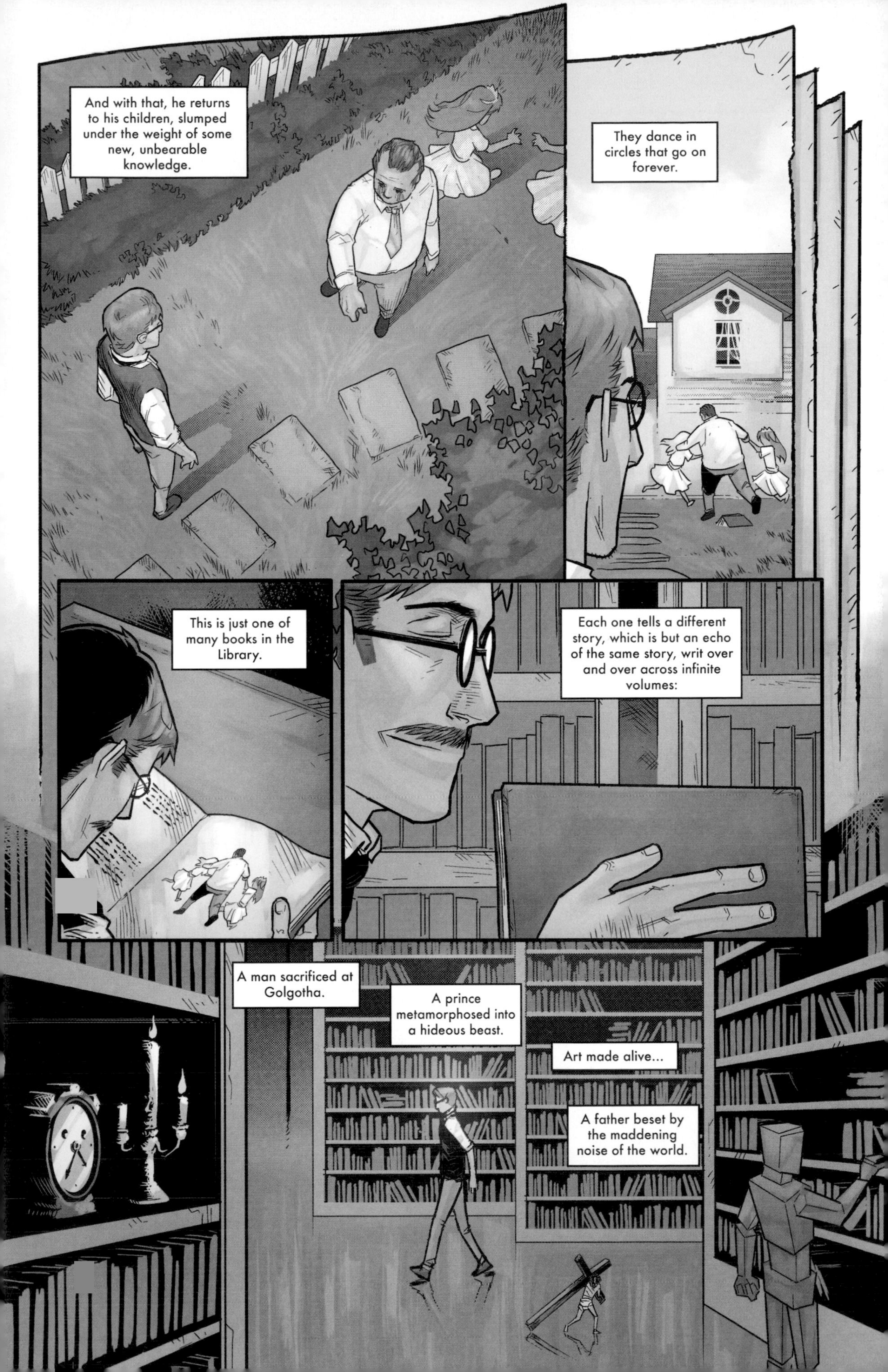
And with that, he returns to his children, slumped under the weight of some new, unbearable knowledge.
They dance in circles that go on forever.
This is just one of many books in the Library.
Each one tells a different story, which is but an echo of the same story, writ over and over across infinite volumes:
A man sacrificed at Golgotha.
A prince metamorphosed into a hideous beast.
Art made alive...
A father beset by the maddening noise of the world.

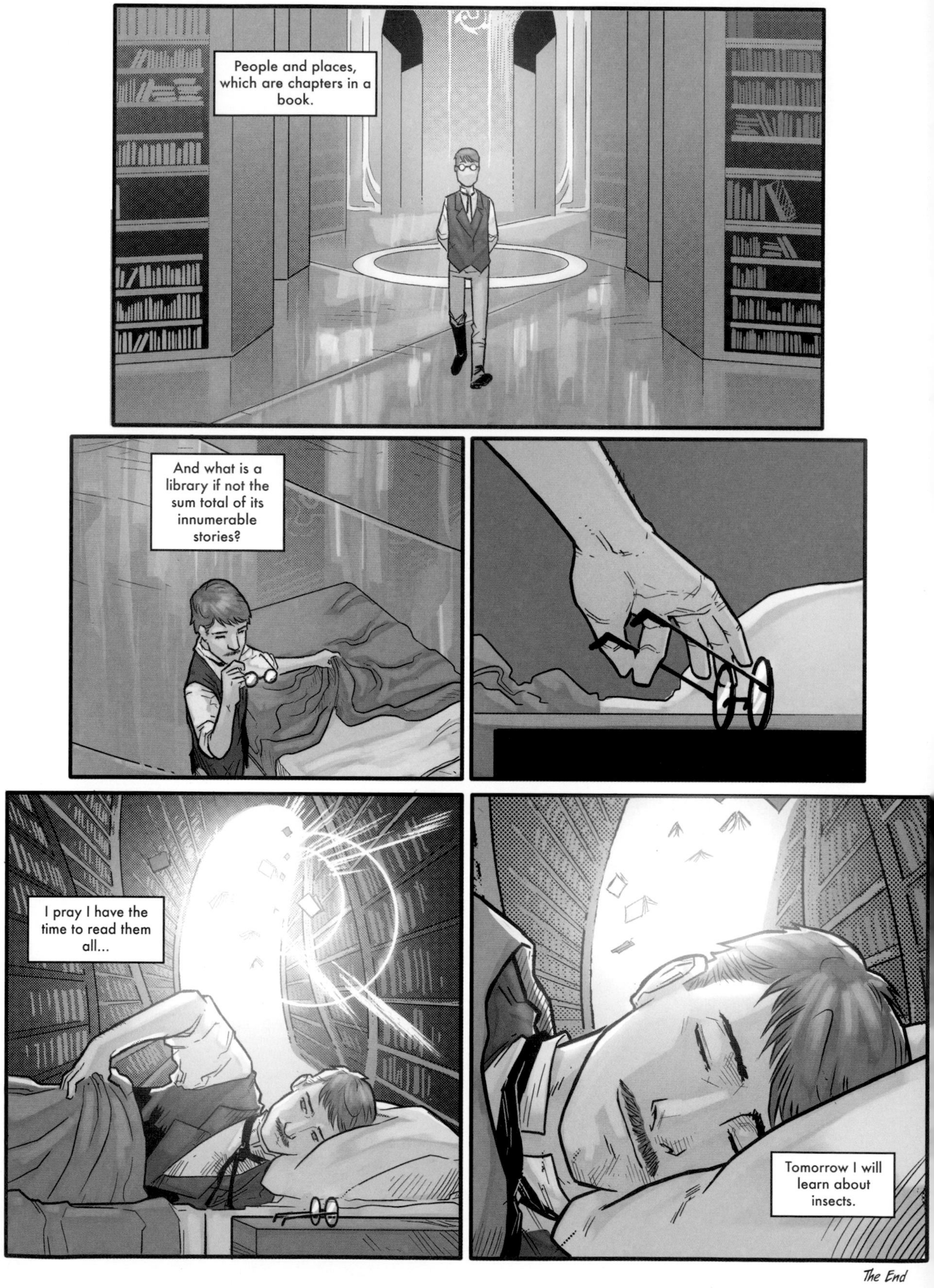
People and places, which are chapters in a book.
And what is a library if not the sum total of its innumerable stories?
I pray I have the time to read them all...
Tomorrow I will learn about insects.

The End

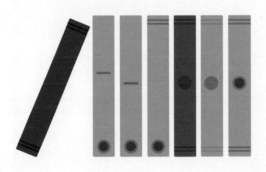

FRIDAY

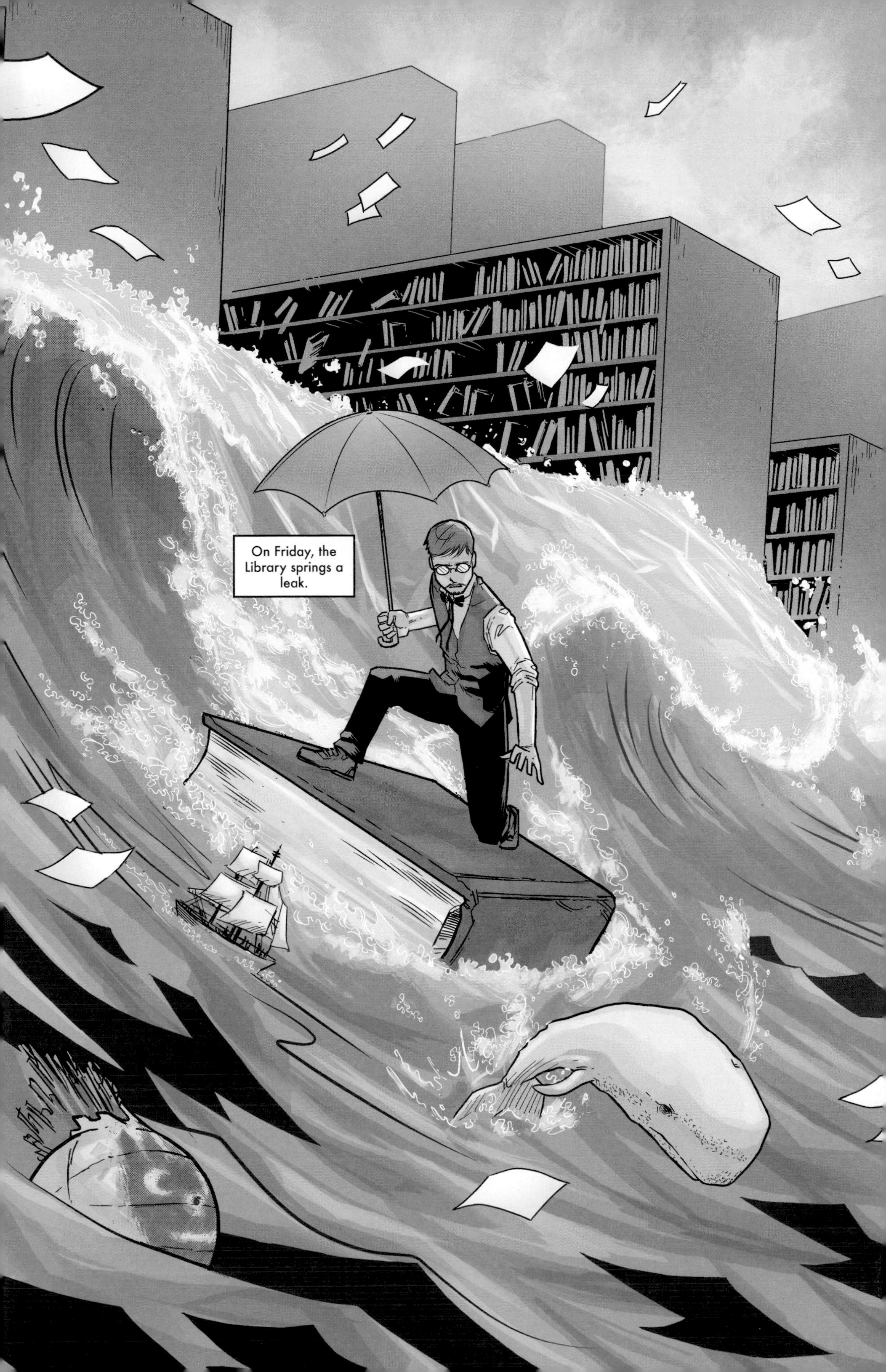
On Friday, the Library springs a leak.

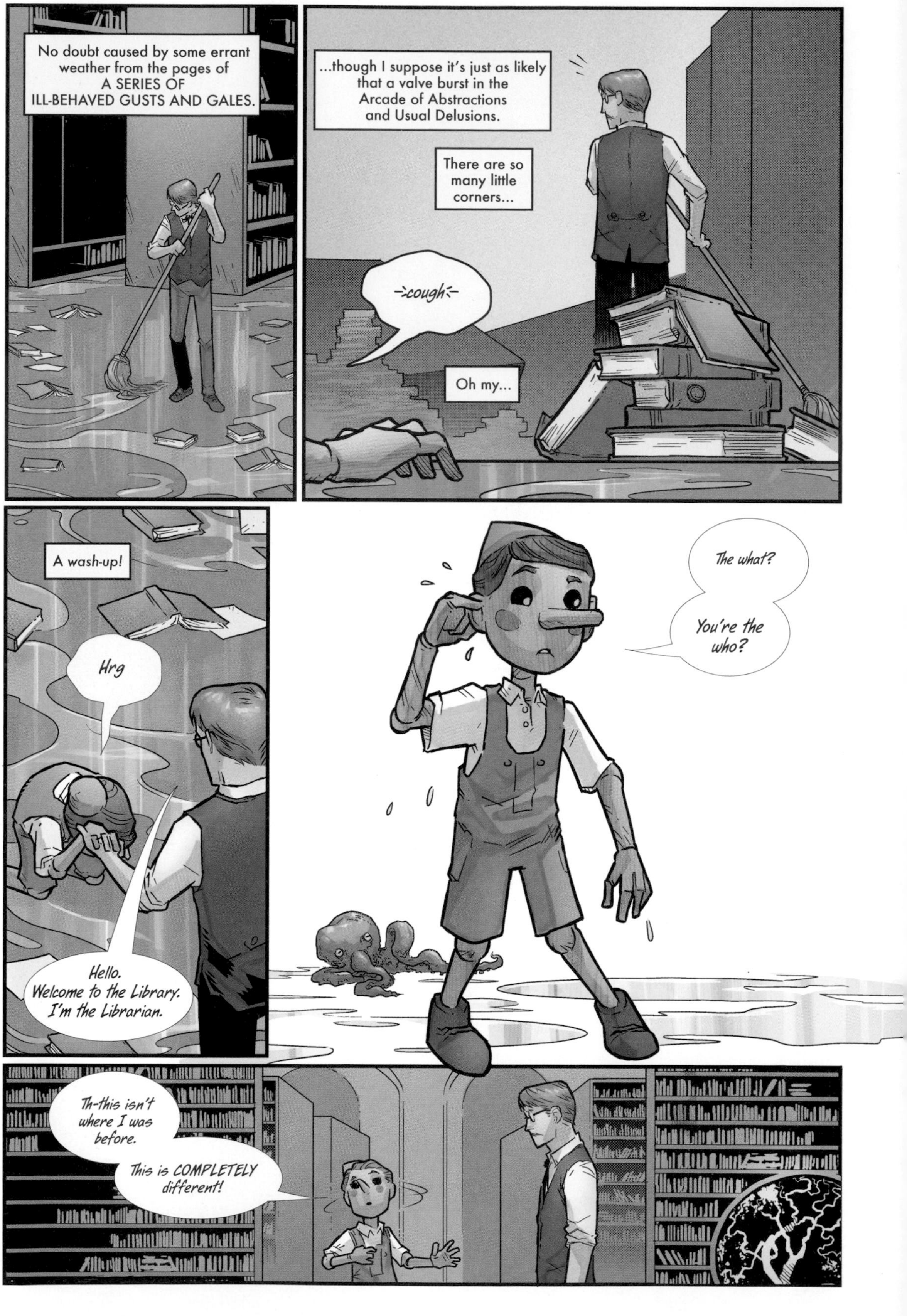
No doubt caused by some errant weather from the pages of A SERIES OF ILL-BEHAVED GUSTS AND GALES.
...though I suppose it's just as likely that a valve burst in the Arcade of Abstractions and Usual Delusions.
There are so many little corners...
-cough-
Oh my...
A wash-up!
Hrg
Hello. Welcome to the Library. I'm the Librarian.
The what?
You're the who?
Th-this isn't where I was before.
This is COMPLETELY different!

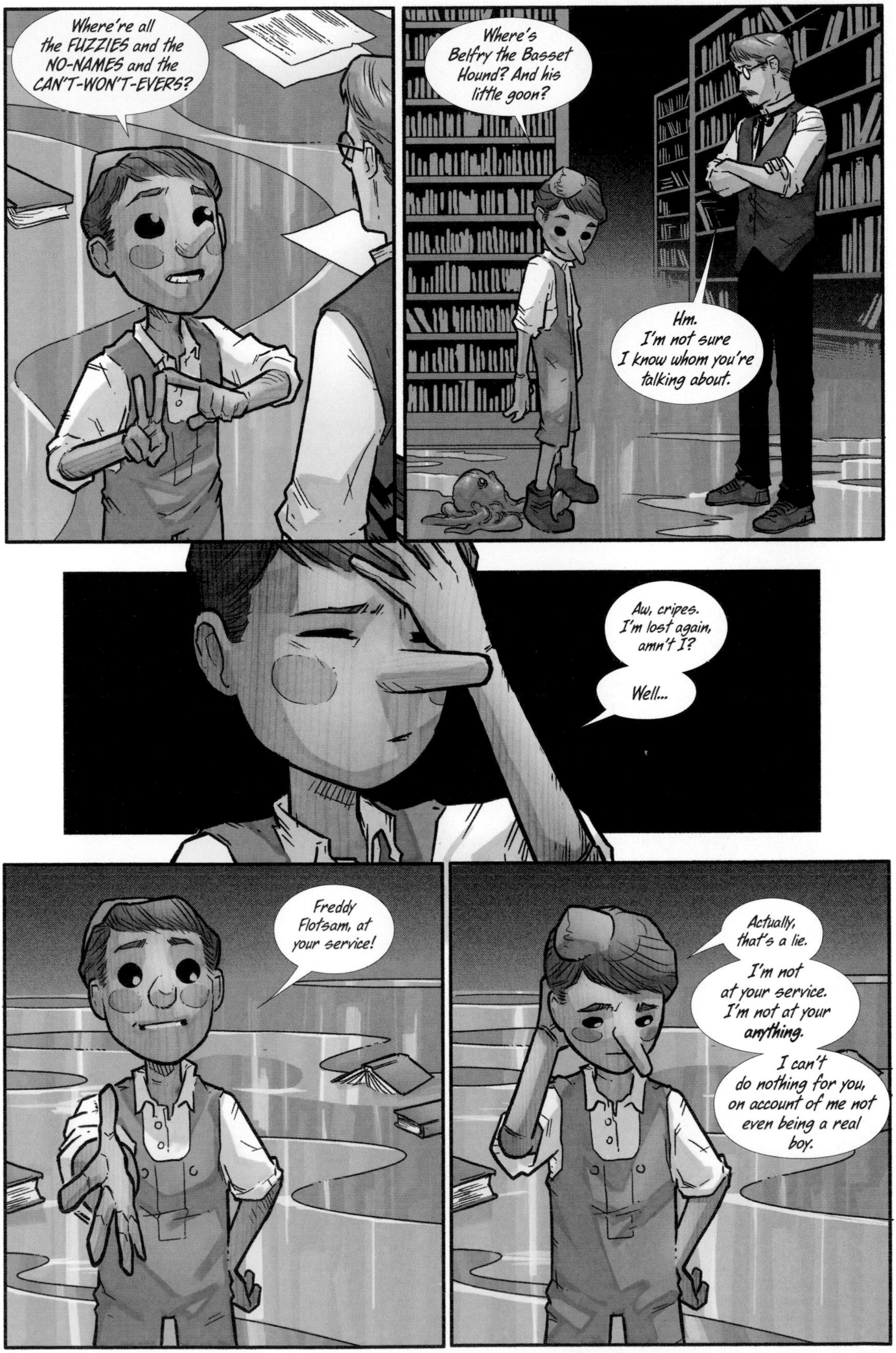
Where're all the FUZZIES and the NO-NAMES and the CAN'T-WON'T-EVERS?
Where's Belfry the Basset Hound? And his little goon?
Hm. I'm not sure I know whom you're talking about.
Aw, cripes. I'm lost again, amn't I?
Well...
Freddy Flotsam, at your service!
Actually, that's a lie.
I'm not at your service. I'm not at your **anything**.
I can't do nothing for you, on account of me not even being a real boy.

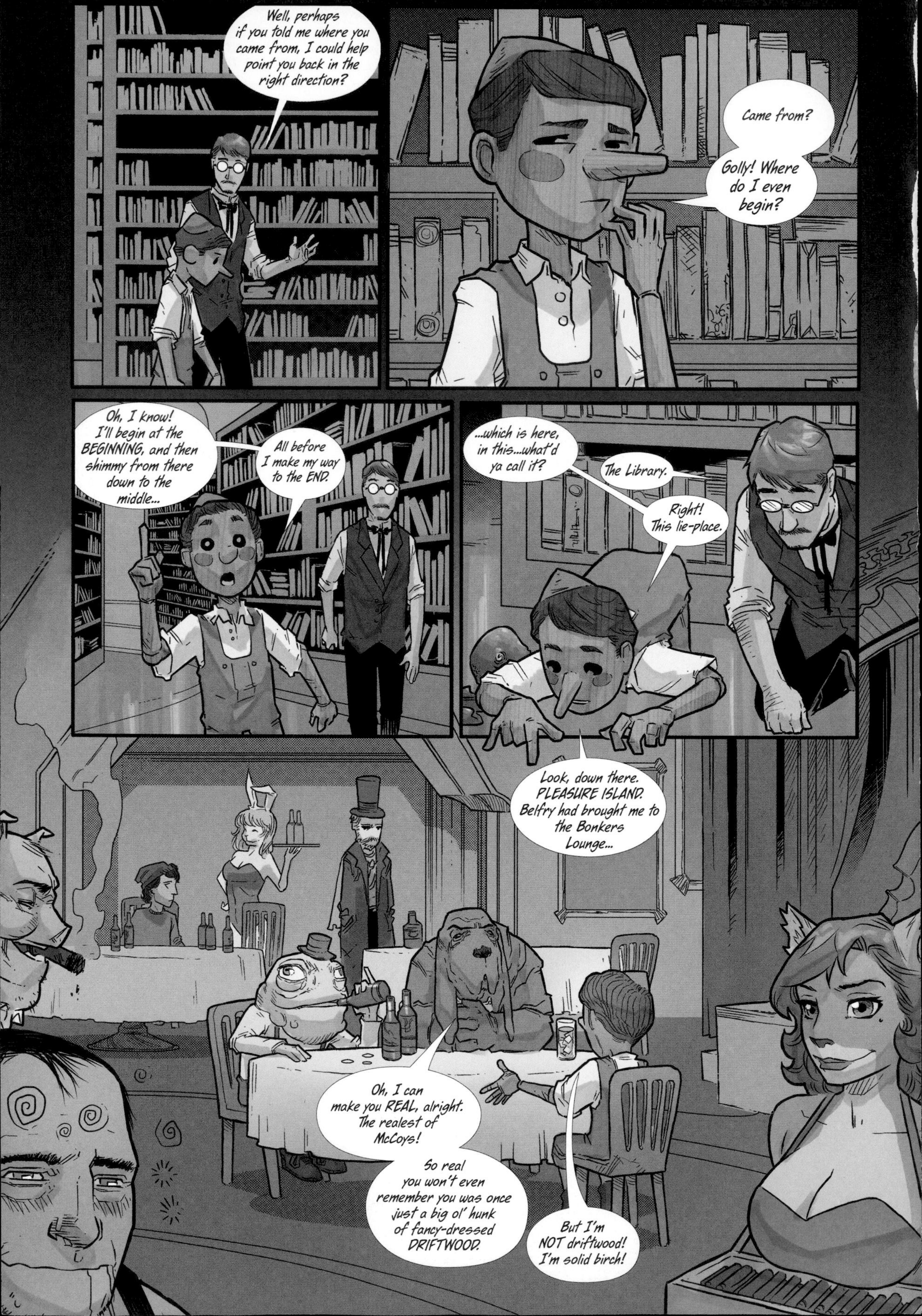
Well, perhaps if you told me where you came from, I could help point you back in the right direction?
Came from?
Golly! Where do I even begin?
Oh, I know! I'll begin at the BEGINNING, and then shimmy from there down to the middle...
All before I make my way to the END.
...which is here, in this...what'd ya call it?
The Library.
Right! This lie-place.
Look, down there. PLEASURE ISLAND. Belfry had brought me to the Bonkers Lounge...
Oh, I can make you REAL, alright. The realest of McCoys!
So real you won't even remember you was once just a big ol' hunk of fancy-dressed DRIFTWOOD.
But I'm NOT driftwood! I'm solid birch!

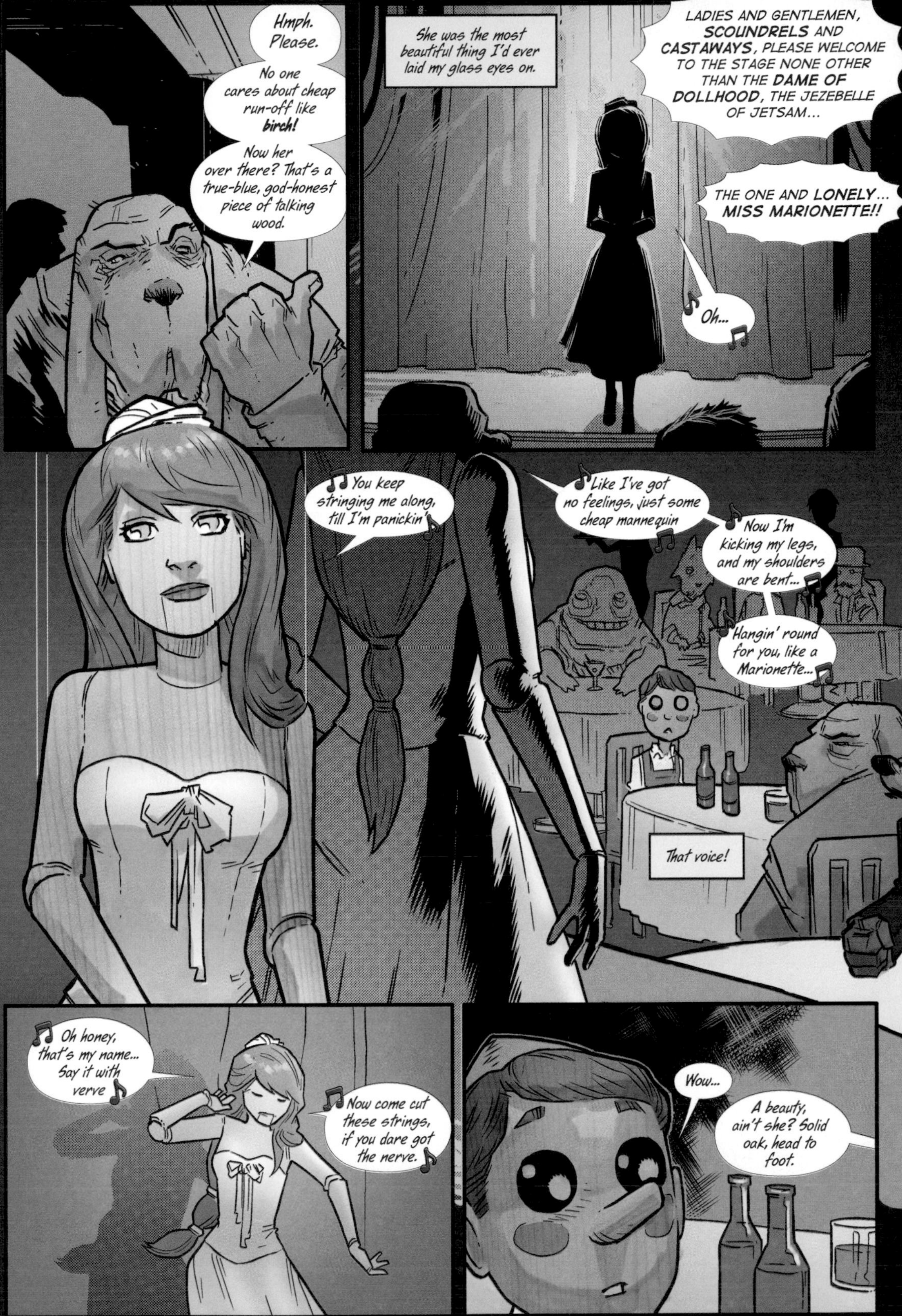
Hmph. Please.
No one cares about cheap run-off like birch!
Now her over there? That's a true-blue, god-honest piece of talking wood.
She was the most beautiful thing I'd ever laid my glass eyes on.
LADIES AND GENTLEMEN, SCOUNDRELS AND CASTAWAYS, PLEASE WELCOME TO THE STAGE NONE OTHER THAN THE DAME OF DOLLHOOD, THE JEZEBELLE OF JETSAM...
THE ONE AND LONELY... MISS MARIONETTE!!
Oh...
You keep stringing me along, till I'm panickin'
Like I've got no feelings, just some cheap mannequin
Now I'm kicking my legs, and my shoulders are bent...
Hangin' round for you, like a Marionette...
That voice!
Oh honey, that's my name... Say it with verve
Now come cut these strings, if you dare got the nerve.
Wow...
A beauty, ain't she? Solid oak, head to foot.

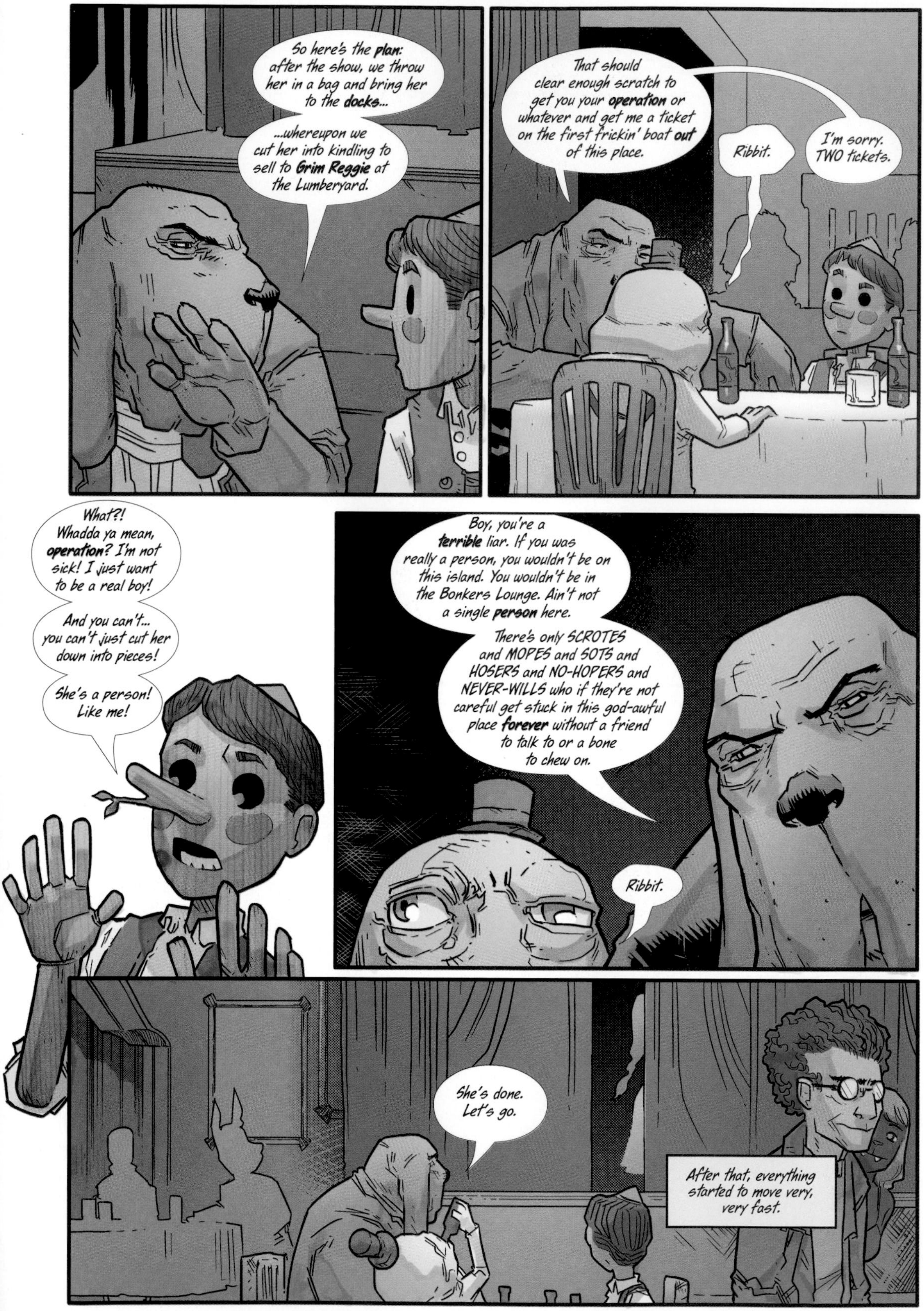
So here's the **plan**: after the show, we throw her in a bag and bring her to the **docks**...
...whereupon we cut her into kindling to sell to **Grim Reggie** at the Lumberyard.
That should clear enough scratch to get you your **operation** or whatever and get me a ticket on the first frickin' boat **out** of this place.
Ribbit.
I'm sorry. TWO tickets.
What?! Whadda ya mean, **operation**? I'm not sick! I just want to be a real boy!
And you can't... you can't just cut her down into pieces!
She's a person! Like me!
Boy, you're a **terrible** liar. If you was really a person, you wouldn't be on this island. You wouldn't be in the Bonkers Lounge. Ain't not a single **person** here.
There's only SCROTES and MOPES and SOTS and HOSERS and NO-HOPERS and NEVER-WILLS who if they're not careful get stuck in this god-awful place **forever** without a friend to talk to or a bone to chew on.
Ribbit.
She's done. Let's go.
After that, everything started to move very, very fast.

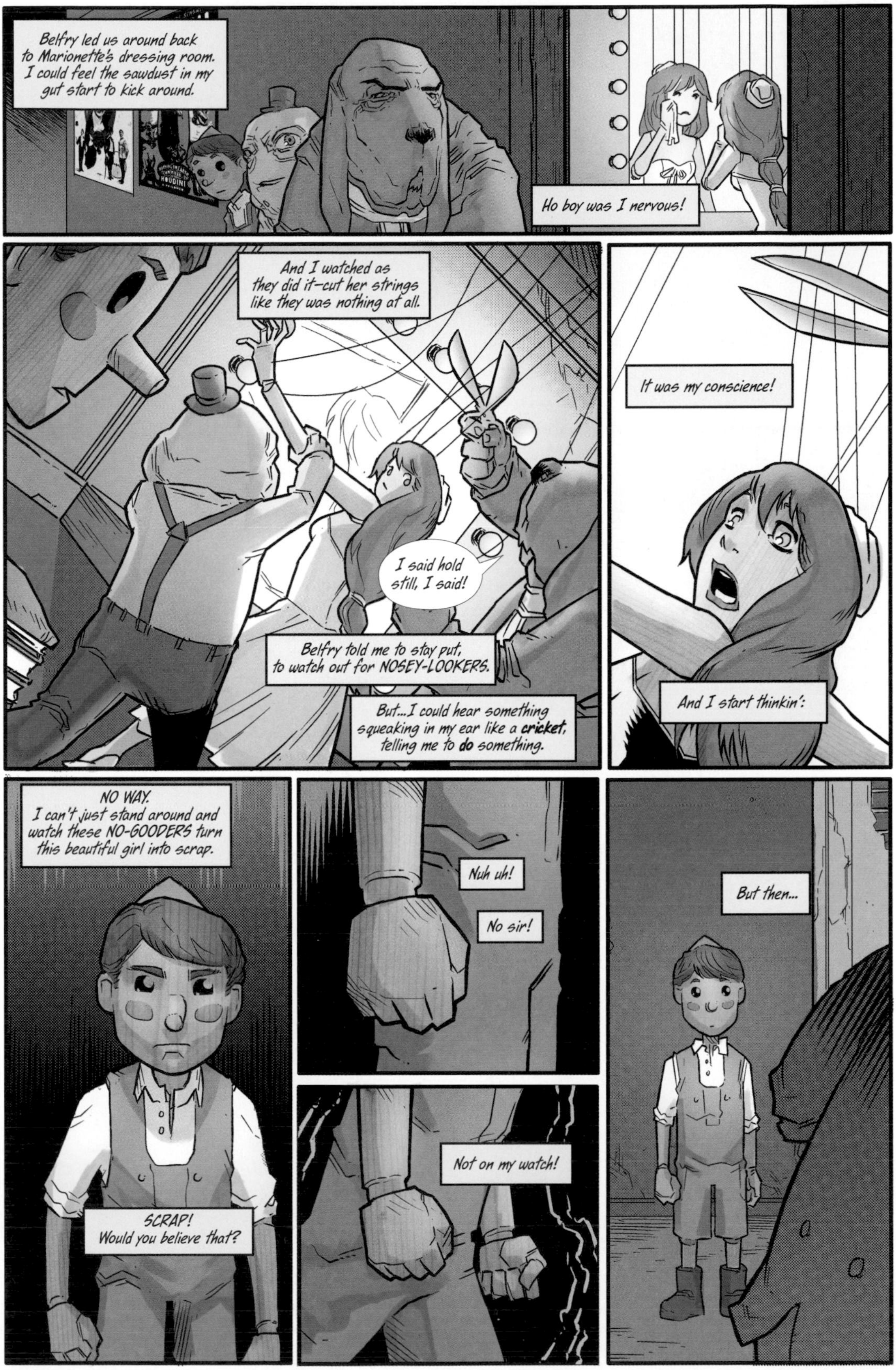
Belfry led us around back to Marionette's dressing room. I could feel the sawdust in my gut start to kick around.
HOUDINI
Ho boy was I nervous!
And I watched as they did it—cut her strings like they was nothing at all.
I said hold still, I said!
Belfry told me to stay put, to watch out for NOSEY-LOOKERS.
But...I could hear something squeaking in my ear like a **cricket**, telling me to **do** something.
It was my conscience!
And I start thinkin':
NO WAY. I can't just stand around and watch these NO-GOODERS turn this beautiful girl into scrap.
SCRAP! Would you believe that?
Nuh uh!
No sir!
Not on my watch!
But then...

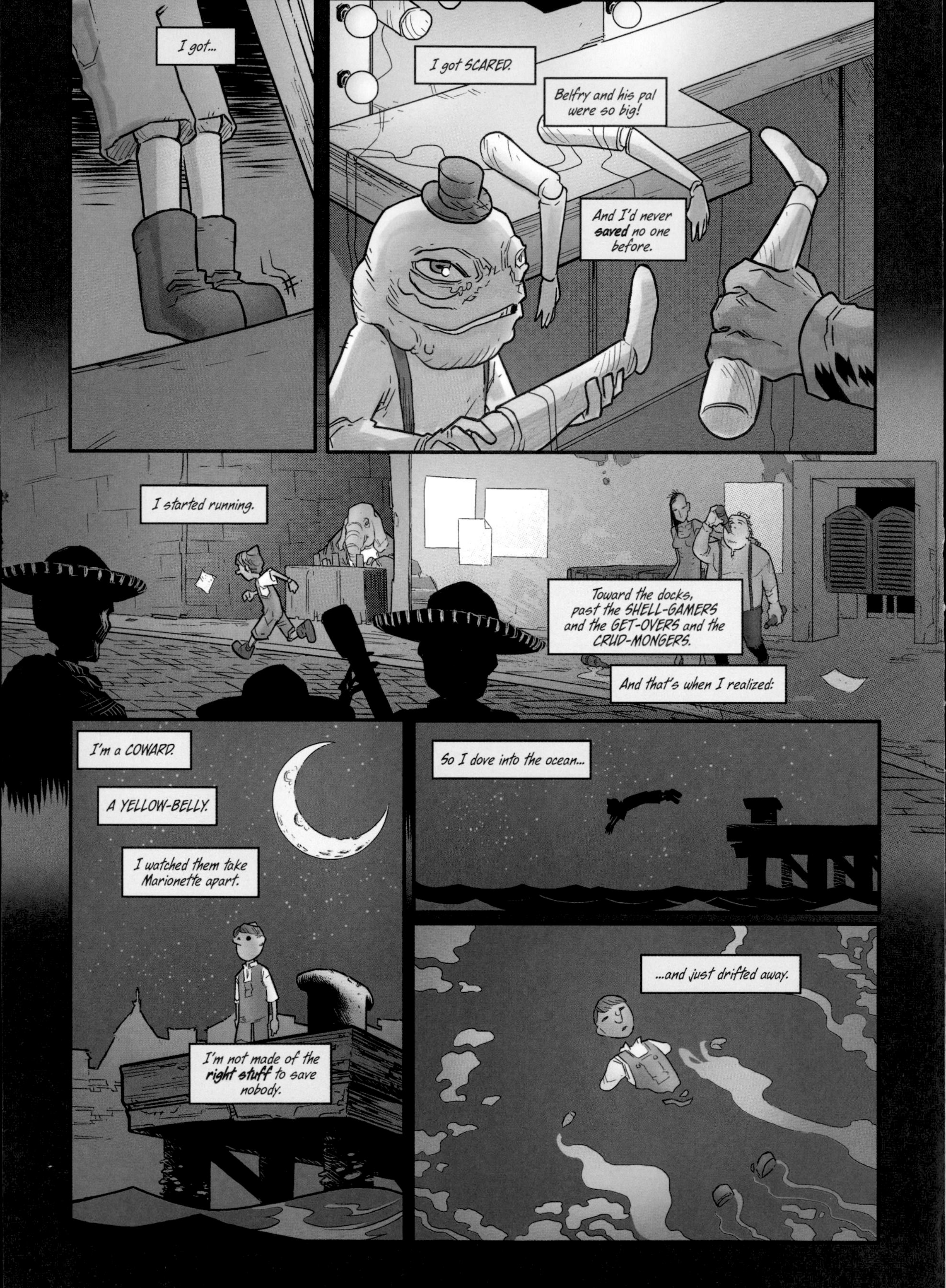

I got...
I got SCARED.
Belfry and his pal were so big!
And I'd never saved no one before.
I started running.
Toward the docks, past the SHELL-GAMERS and the GET-OVERS and the CRUD-MONGERS.
And that's when I realized:
I'm a COWARD.
A YELLOW-BELLY.
I watched them take Marionette apart.
I'm not made of the right stuff to save nobody.
So I dove into the ocean...
...and just drifted away.

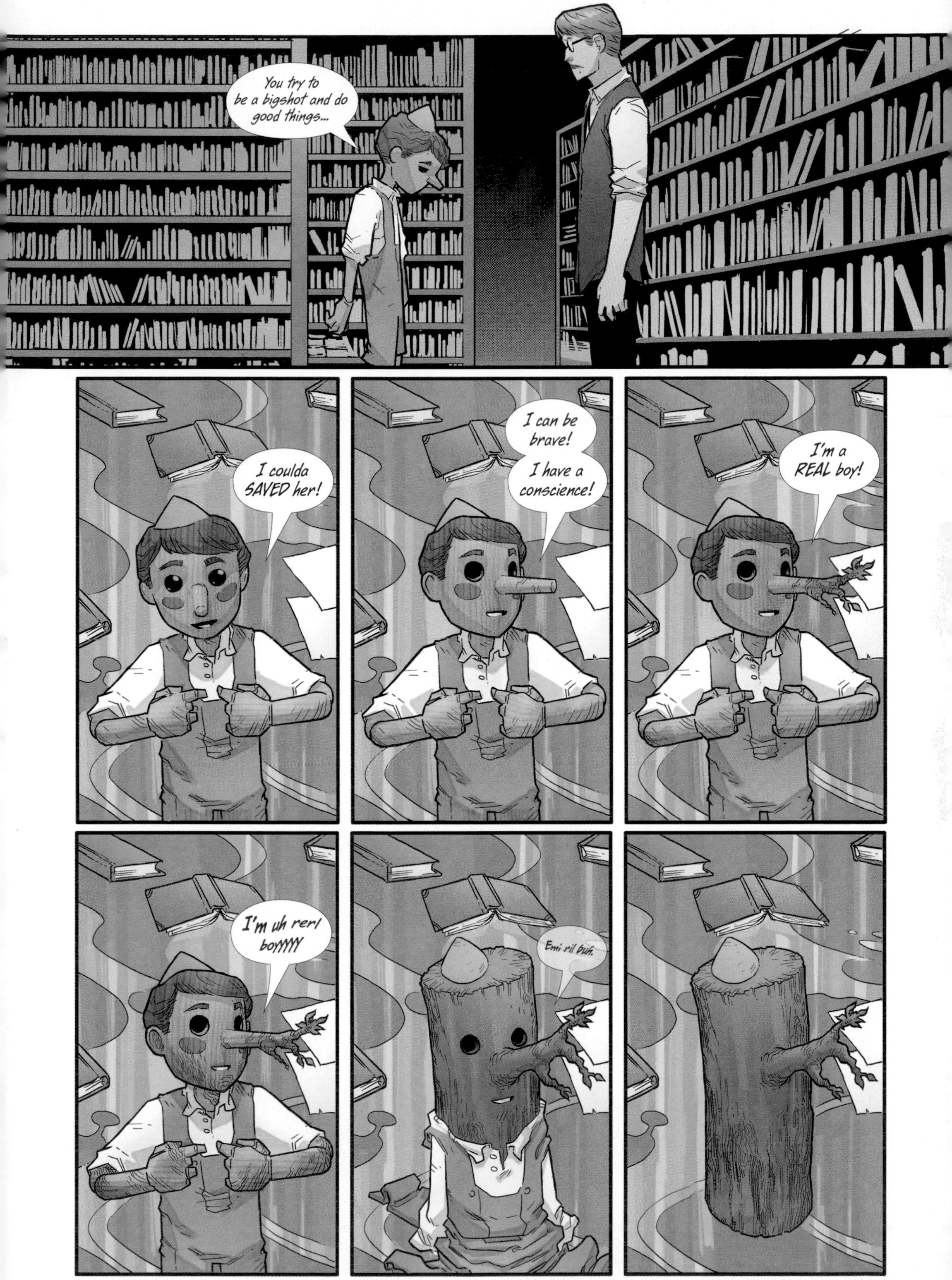
You try to be a bigshot and do good things...
I coulda SAVED her!
I can be brave!
I have a conscience!
I'm a REAL boy!
I'm uh rerl boyyyyy
Emi ril buh.

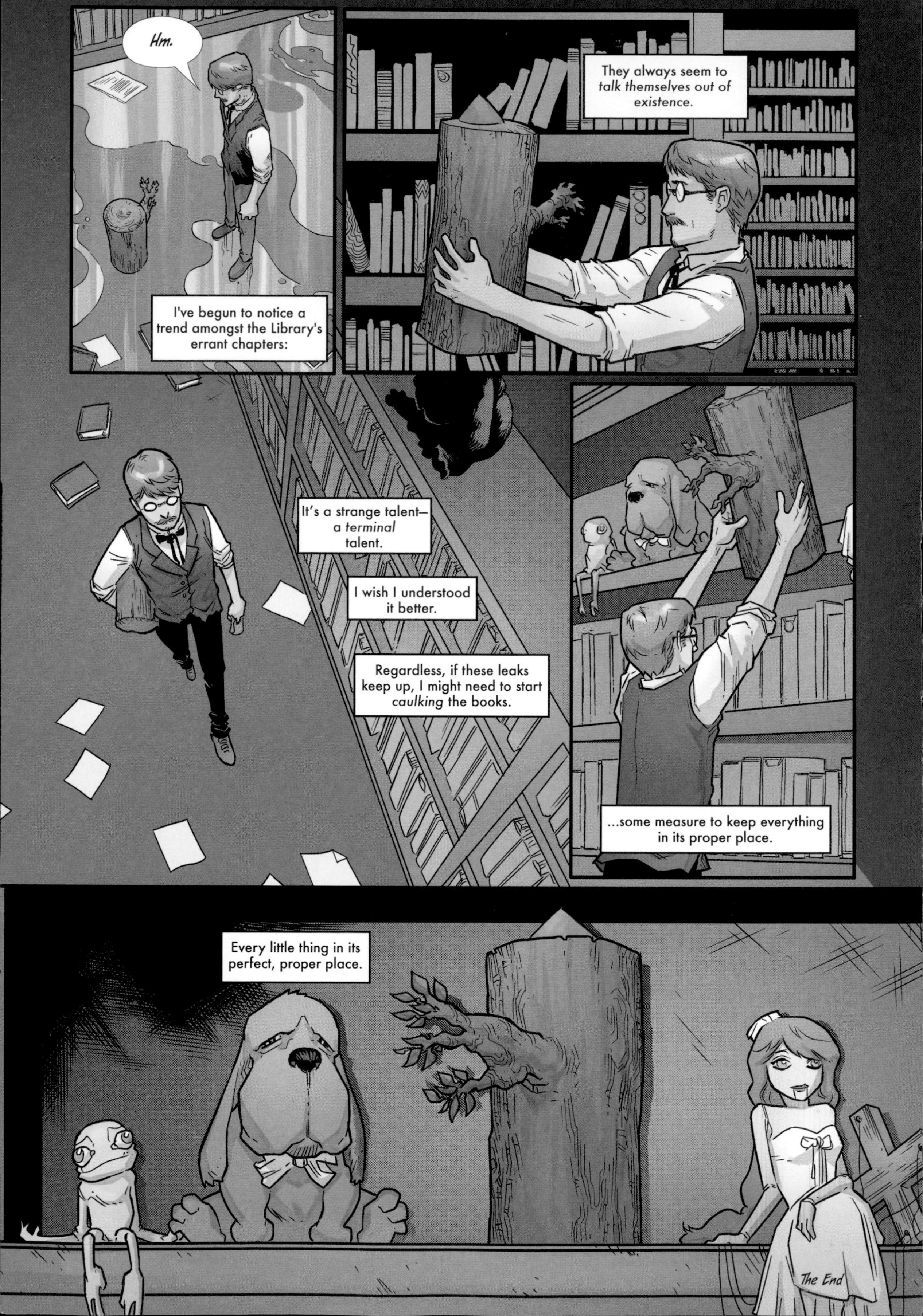
Hm.
I've begun to notice a trend amongst the Library's errant chapters:
They always seem to *talk themselves* out of existence.
It's a strange talent— a *terminal* talent.
I wish I understood it better.
Regardless, if these leaks keep up, I might need to start *caulking* the books.
...some measure to keep everything in its proper place.
Every little thing in its perfect, proper place.
The End

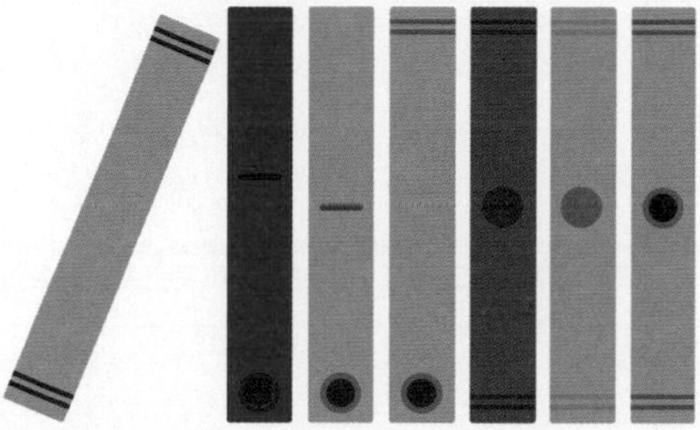

SATURDAY

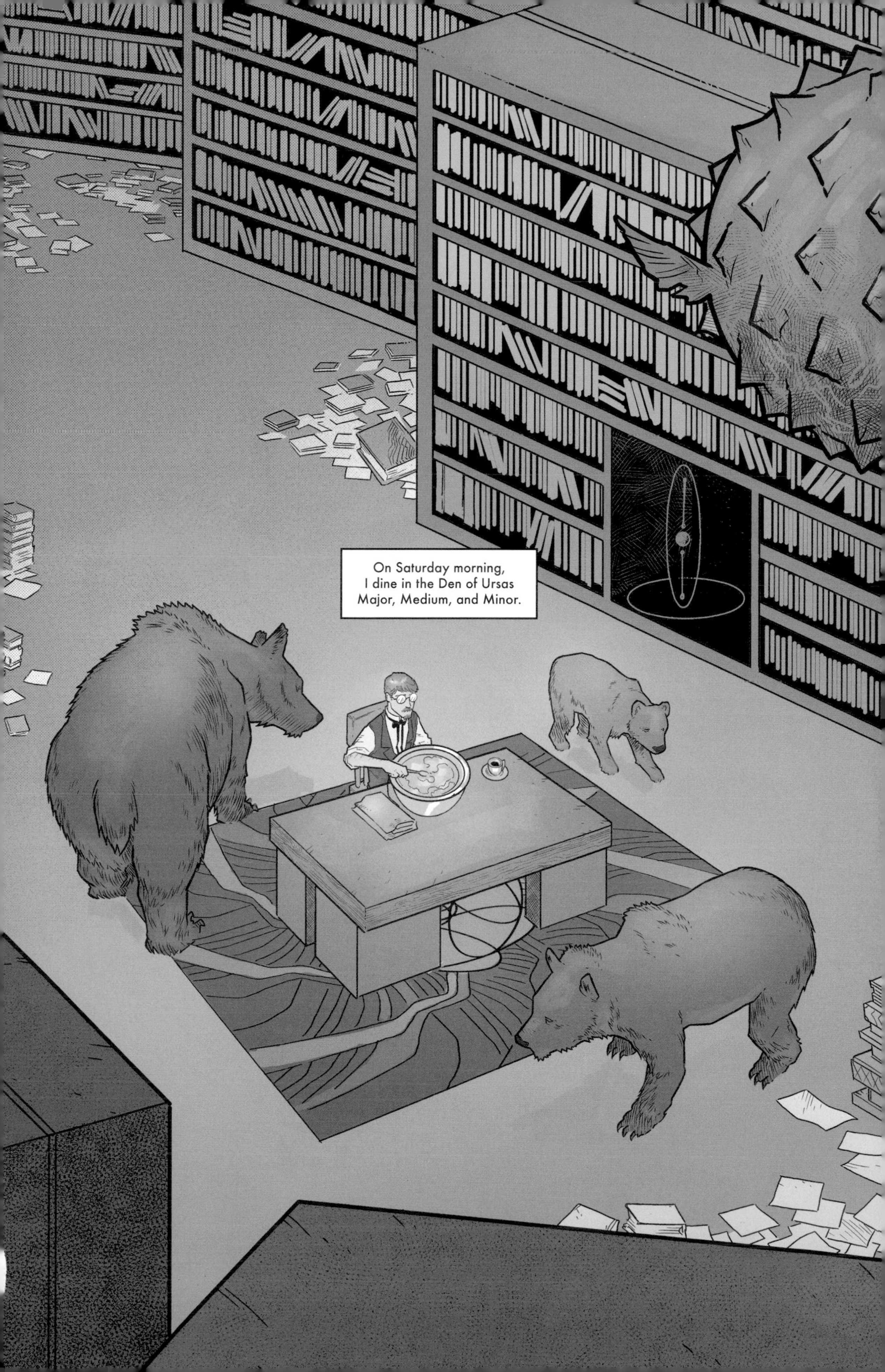
On Saturday morning, I dine in the Den of Ursas Major, Medium, and Minor.

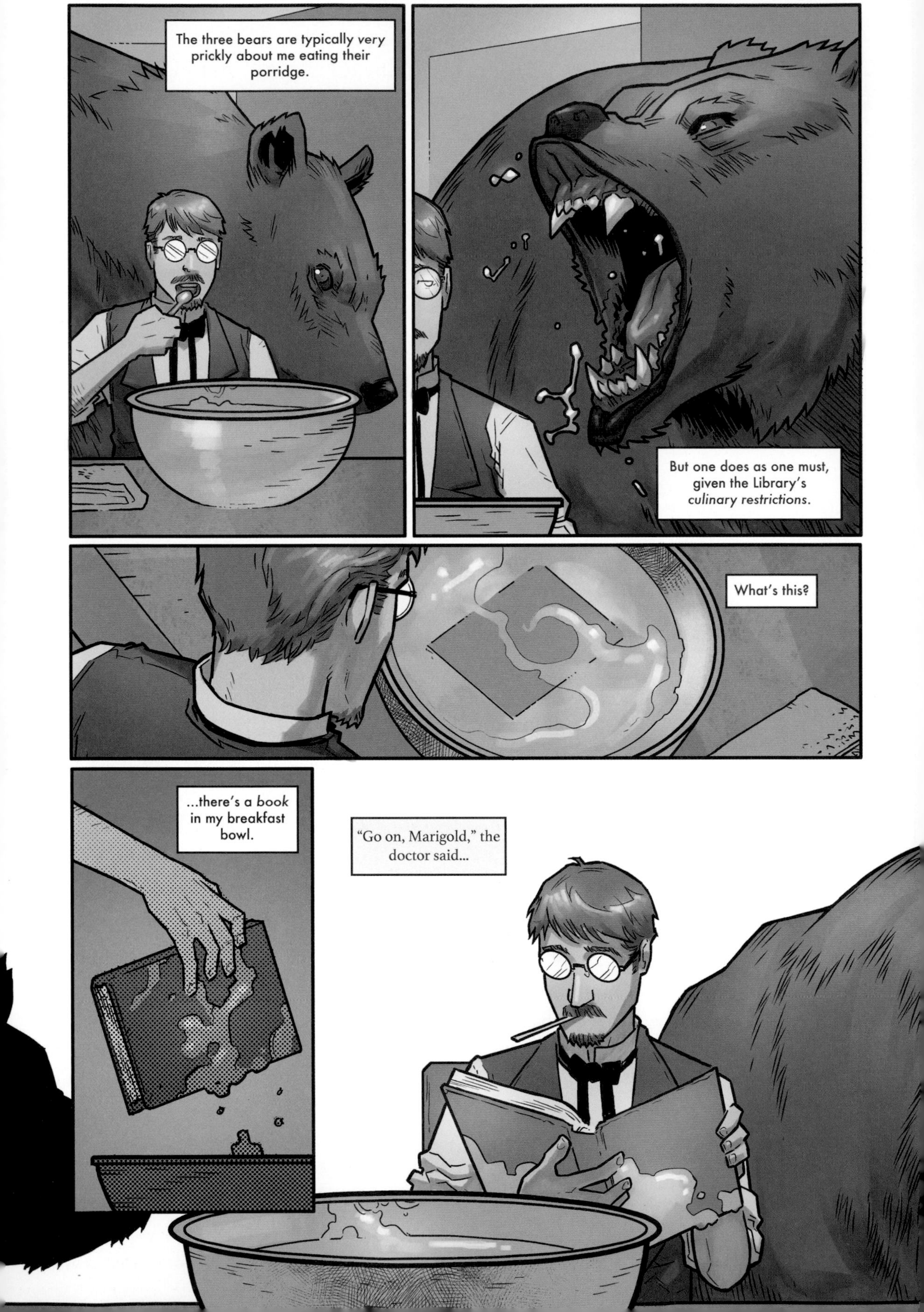

The three bears are typically *very* prickly about me eating their porridge.
But one does as one must, given the Library's *culinary restrictions*.
What's this?
...there's a *book* in my breakfast bowl.
"Go on, Marigold," the doctor said...

PART ONE

"Go on, Marigold," the doctor said. He had this way of talking out of the side of his face. "Tell me more."

What exactly did he want her to say? Did he want to hear how she hadn't slept in three days? That her tongue felt gigantic inside her mouth? That for a week now she'd been generally zonked and lethargic and constantly a few feet back of her own head? (Just yesterday she had somehow *watched* herself walk across the street; it was only after the light turned red that her eyes finally caught up with her body.) Upshot was: the Lexapro wasn't doing any good.

She pressed herself into the couch and played with the gauze covering her knuckles.

"You know, it's not uncommon to have to try a few different kinds before you find the one that's right for you," the doctor said. "Antidepressants can be tricky."

Tricky. Oh wow, great. Perfect. Here's a thing that's also tricky: having your head enveloped in a chemical fog, so much so that on your last shift at the shop you accidentally poured piping hot coffee two inches to the left of the cup, directly onto the back of your left hand, and had to be rushed to the ER for scalds and treated with a burn cream that smells, in fact, not very pleasant at all, and has to be reapplied under the gauze once every twelve hours for seven days.

And this injury, of course, prevents you from working more shifts until it (the hand) is fully healed, much to the chagrin of your boss, who is already shall we say less than pleased with your performance,

having said in earshot on more than one occasion: *What is with her, anyway?*

There's the issue of money, too, and being more or less out of it.

The doctor took out his blue pad. "I want you to try fluoxetine. Prozac. It has a pretty low adverse effect profile. Some nausea, maybe a weird dream or two." He scribbled and tore off a sheet. "I haven't had too many patients lose sleep on Prozac. Give it a few weeks and let's see if it takes."

She got to her apartment and started an internal vocabulary list. This was her little trick, something she employed to calm down and make herself feel better. Though sometimes it made her feel worse.

Conflagration, *nefarious*, *insipid*, *ascetic*, *reprove*. *Abscond*, *exonerate*, *ineffable*, *indelible*, *inscrutable*. *Vestige*, *visage*, *veracity*, *inveterate*, *invariably*…

She could find infinite space inside a word, space in which to fit herself perfectly. Each string of letters was like its own little cozy chair. Or casket.

Later, she called Gary, because she knew he'd be home—he was always home, on account of not having a job or any other friends. He was also far and away the horniest little dweeb she'd ever known.

"Hi, Gary," Marigold said.

"Goldie!"

"Can I come over?" she asked.

"Sure, but I'm out of rubbers—can you pick some up?"

PART TWO

....

After ten minutes or so, he pulled out.

"Ah, shit," Gary said.

"What is it?" Marigold asked.

"Shit fucking shit."

"What is it?"

"This friggin' medication I'm on. Cymbalta. It makes it, like, impossible to cum. My dick is just totally busted."

She'd barely noticed. "Do you like it?" she asked.

"A busted pecker? Why the friggin' heck would I like that?"

"No, I mean the Cymbalta, the medicine. Does it work for you?"

"Oh," Gary said, rubbing the back of his neck, "I think so, but it's hard to tell." He pulled his condom off and flicked it across the room. "I know it's supposed to make me happier, but most of the time I just end up feeling kind of, like, you know, sleepy? Like in the middle of the day, out of nowhere, I'll need to sit down and take a nap. You ever get tired like that?"

She did. All the time.

"And it's hell on my stomach," he said. "You don't even want to know."

That was true: she really didn't want to know.

"But I don't think about offing myself anymore," he said.

A year ago, he'd been institutionalized for a full month after locking himself in the bathroom with a toaster. Marigold had visited him twice, and both times he tried to get her to go down on him in the Arts & Crafts closet.

He clarified: "Well, I don't think about it as much. Not the way I used to. It's still there, you know, but not as, I guess...*loud*. So that's, like, good. Right?"

With that, Gary turned over and instantly fell asleep. But Marigold couldn't shut down for the life of her. She focused at a point on the ceiling and thought: *spandrel*, *mullion*, *gait*, *mien*, *nascent*, *codified*, *posit*, *trope*. *Respite*, *repast*, *redolent*, *recondite*, and eventually, after a while, she drifted off.

She dreamt, as she often dreamt, that she was in the circus. She walked on a wire way above everything. The crowd, a hundred feet down, sat silently and gawked straight up in awe. Or maybe not. Maybe they roared and clapped their hands madly in anticipation. It didn't matter either way. What mattered was the show: her, Marigold the Magnificent, displaying a rare aptitude for balance, prancing nonchalantly across a tightrope while a trapeze act—a set of androgynous twins— swung past her vision, just to the left. Down in the ring, the ringmaster sashayed a whip from side to side, leading by the nose first a tiger, then a baby elephant, and finally a trio of bears—all of whom were wearing tutus, which in the context of the dream, felt just about right.

Then in came a car, a really small one. Out of it poured twenty, maybe thirty clowns. Some of them honked these little horns, while others did cartwheels. A few squirted water guns into the crowd. The clowns laughed and the beskirted animals danced and up in the different atmosphere with the highflying, genderless twins, Marigold felt absolutely invincible. She was awake and present and to hell with her moods and medicines. To hell with Mom and her new boyfriend Rick. To hell with Rick and the way he'd rub her thigh on the couch when Mom wasn't looking, sometimes yelling into the kitchen, "Well golly, Lorna, haven't you just the sweetest sort of daughter."

No, up here things were hi-def clear. No fuzz or fog or anything. Complete vacancy of mind. She was *just right*.

The alarm buzzer woke her. It was time to change the gauze.

A few days later, she called Gary, but it wasn't Gary who answered the phone. It took her about half a minute to register the stranger on the other end's voice—the Prozac had been delaying all of her audio-visual input, feeding the world to her thirty seconds too late. It was like a live broadcast of life from somewhere just slightly remote.

After some silence, she finally heard: "Who is this? Is it about the service?"

The voice, she discovered, belonged to Gary's grandmother, who explained the previous day's proceedings like this:

Gary, having just finished a shower, walked, wearing only a towel around his hips, through the house from his room to the garage. There, he retrieved a spool of bungee, which he used to make a noose. He took the noose back to his room, closed the door, and, standing on a chair, fastened the unknotted end of the bungee to a metal pull-up bar—his father had installed it years ago as a sort of tacit suggestion toward fitness, but Gary only ever used it as a place to hang his dry cleaning.

Pleased with the tensile strength of his contraption, he stuck his head through the noose's loop, and began to masturbate.

It should be noted here that Gary's grandmother, relating all this in a tone Marigold could only describe as *phlegmatic*, or else *stolid* or *dispassionate* or *unflappable*, had actually used the phrase "getting himself off," and not, as she'd heard it in the dialogue in her head, "masturbate."

"He climaxed right before the chair gave way," his grandmother said. "Maybe you could call it a happy death. *La petite mort*."

Awestruck, *flabbergasted*, *gobsmacked*, *nonplussed*.

Or maybe she had said "masturbate" after all.

The funeral, it needn't be mentioned, was very, very sad.

PART THREE

It took about twelve days until she started seeing Gary's ghost. She walked into her room one afternoon, and there he was, playing solitaire on her bed with a set of insubstantial cards.

"They really got the name right," Gary's ghost said. "This really is the loneliest game."

Was it the medication? Grief? A true-blue, no-kidding paranormal phenomenon? She of course had no clue, but she did know absolutely that it was good to see his face again, even if it happened to be kind of bluish and see-through. He also had this nasty rope burn around his neck, which he was pointing to.

"Can't believe I did this to myself." It still looked fresh. "You know I went to haunt my house? But I had to leave 'cause my mom wouldn't stop crying. I'm a friggin' jerk, ain't I?"

"Is this real?" Marigold asked. "You're dead, Gary."

"As a doornail," he said. "My dad had to put pants on my body before the coroner showed up. Poor guy."

Stave, *hew*, *lee*, *lassitude*, *panacea*, *acclivity*, *catamite*. It wasn't working—she was sort of freaking out.

"You're haunting *me*, Gary!"

"I know, I know," he said. "But who else is there?"

She had hoped the doctor could help straighten things out. One week full of circus dreams and an apparitional boyfriend only she could see, floating around and talking non-stop about his erections. (Death, it turned out, had little effect on Gary's libido.)

"He's even here right now," she told the doctor. "He's standing right next to you."

"I see," the doctor said. "And how long would you say this has been going on?"

"You ever notice he sort of talks out of the side of his mouth?" Gary's ghost said.

"And what about my dreams?" Marigold asked. "Why is it always a circus?"

"Marigold," the doctor said.

"And are the trapeze artists men or women? Or both? Do antidepressants do this?"

"You're sounding kinda crazy, Goldie,"

Gary's ghost said. "Kind of like you're losing it."

The doctor put his pad aside. "Marigold, I think it's time we consider lithium. What you're exhibiting are the telltale signs of—"

She couldn't hear what he said next. All she heard was a voice from inside that droned *mendicant*, *harridan*, *miasma*, *feckless*, *imbroglio*.

It occurred to her that she might very well be losing it.

How do people do this, she thought. How do you live stuck inside your body, stuck inside your mind?

Gary floated around the office looking for a deck of cards. Each time he passed through the doctor, the man shivered as if struck with a sudden chill.

These minds! We try one thing after another to uncross the wires and still it never makes full sense. SSRIs and cocaine and Better Life seminars and intramural sports and introductory knitting—none of it fixes the root problem. You can never peel back to the very first layer, the one that's mucking up the entire operation.

She looked down and realized her gauze was three days old. Yellow pus was bleeding through to the top.

The doctor talked while Gary cracked wise; Marigold felt as if she was swinging between two realities completely at odds.

Oscillation, *vacillation*, *peristalsis*.

Oh, to be aloft on a tightrope, hovering over the cheering crowd! Yes, it's dangerous. But it's also beautiful: complete vacancy of mind, to hell with the troubles of before and tomorrow.

She raised her head to the doctor and said, "Gary's rummaging through your desk drawers."

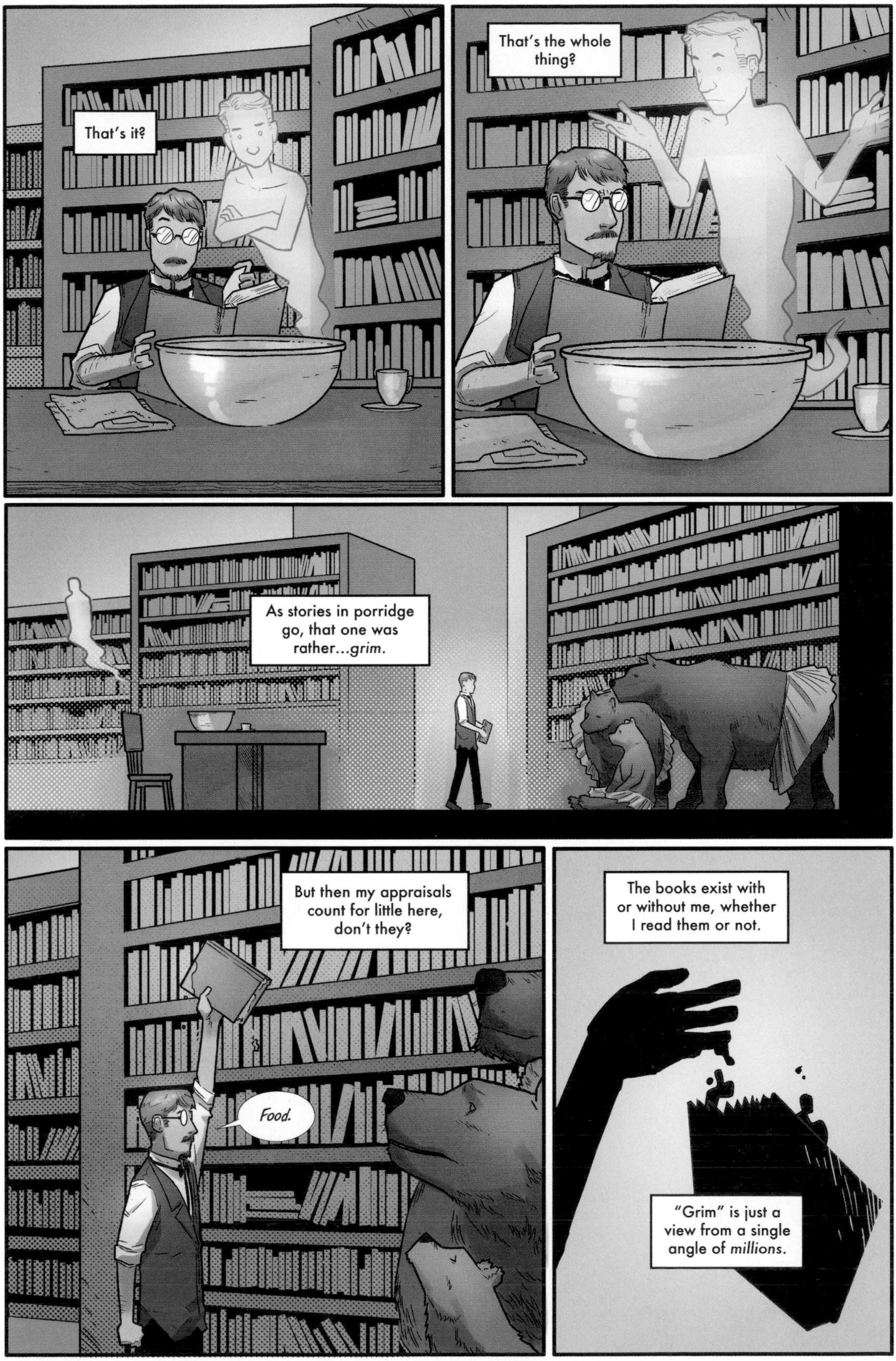
That's it?
That's the whole thing?
As stories in porridge go, that one was rather...*grim*.
But then my appraisals count for little here, don't they?
Food.
The books exist with or without me, whether I read them or not.
"Grim" is just a view from a single angle of *millions*.

Still, I do wonder what happened to poor Marigold.

She seemed very lost.

...or, by virtue of my discovery, was she very *found*?

Marigold.

What a lovely name for a person.

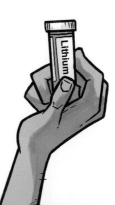

The End

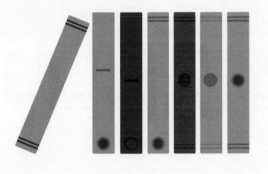

SUNDAY

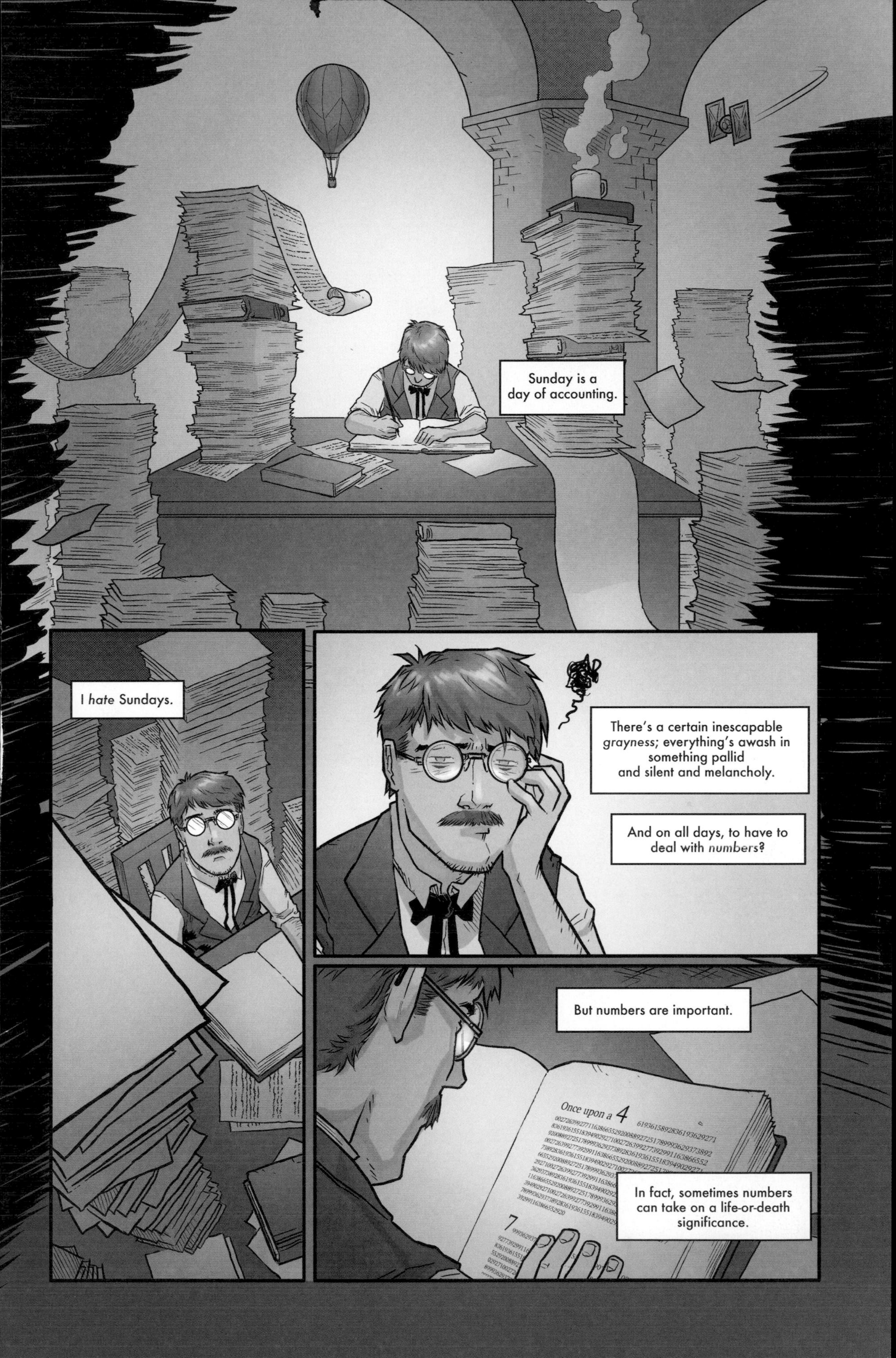
Sunday is a day of accounting.
I *hate* Sundays.
There's a certain inescapable *grayness*; everything's awash in something pallid and silent and melancholy.
And on all days, to have to deal with *numbers*?
But numbers are important.
Once upon a 4
In fact, sometimes numbers can take on a life-or-death significance.

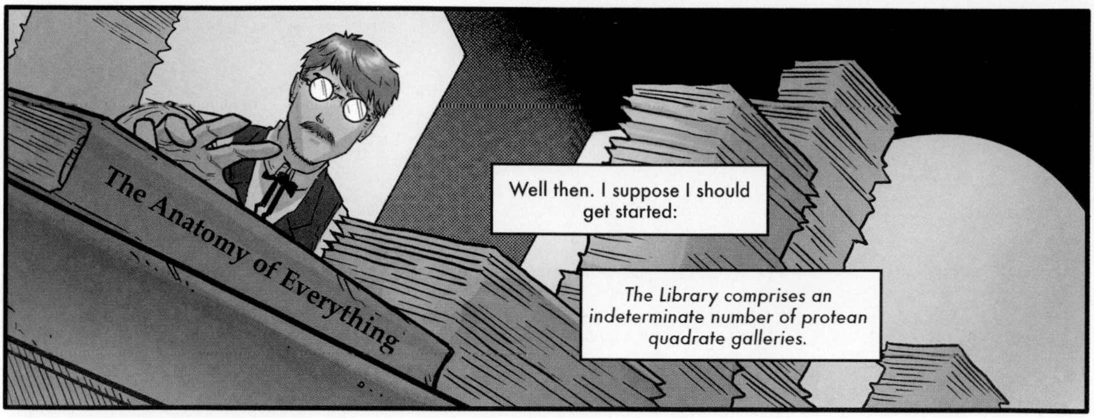
The Anatomy of Everything
Well then. I suppose I should get started:
The Library comprises an indeterminate number of protean quadrate galleries.

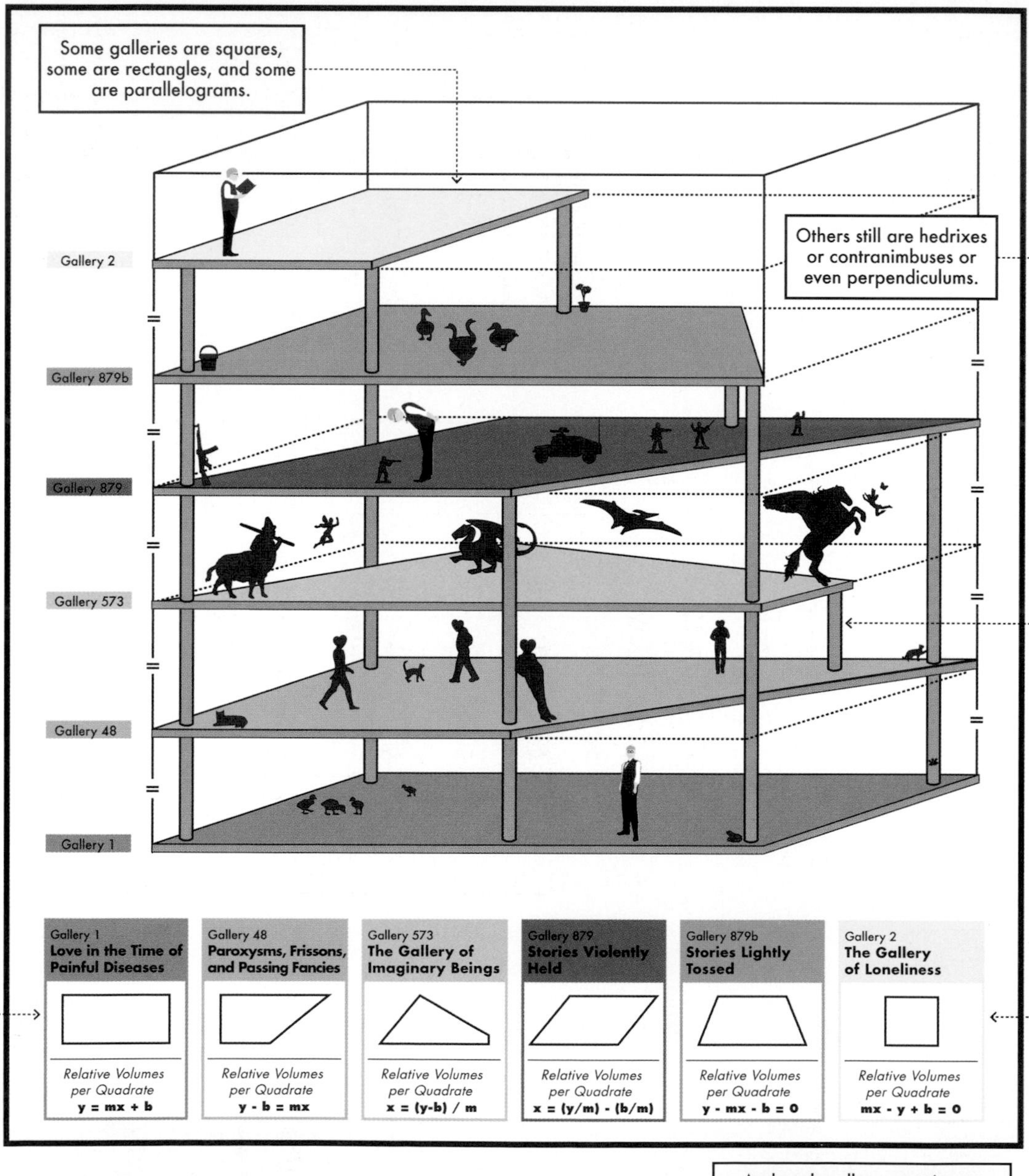
Some galleries are squares, some are rectangles, and some are parallelograms.
Others still are hedrixes or contranimbuses or even perpendiculums.
Gallery 2
Gallery 879b
Gallery 879
Gallery 573
Gallery 48
Gallery 1
Gallery 1
Love in the Time of Painful Diseases
Relative Volumes per Quadrate
y = mx + b
Gallery 48
Paroxysms, Frissons, and Passing Fancies
Relative Volumes per Quadrate
y - b = mx
Gallery 573
The Gallery of Imaginary Beings
Relative Volumes per Quadrate
x = (y-b) / m
Gallery 879
Stories Violently Held
Relative Volumes per Quadrate
x = (y/m) - (b/m)
Gallery 879b
Stories Lightly Tossed
Relative Volumes per Quadrate
y - mx - b = 0
Gallery 2
The Gallery of Loneliness
Relative Volumes per Quadrate
mx - y + b = 0

And each gallery contains an unknowable but nonetheless equal amount of books, held on an equal number of shelves.

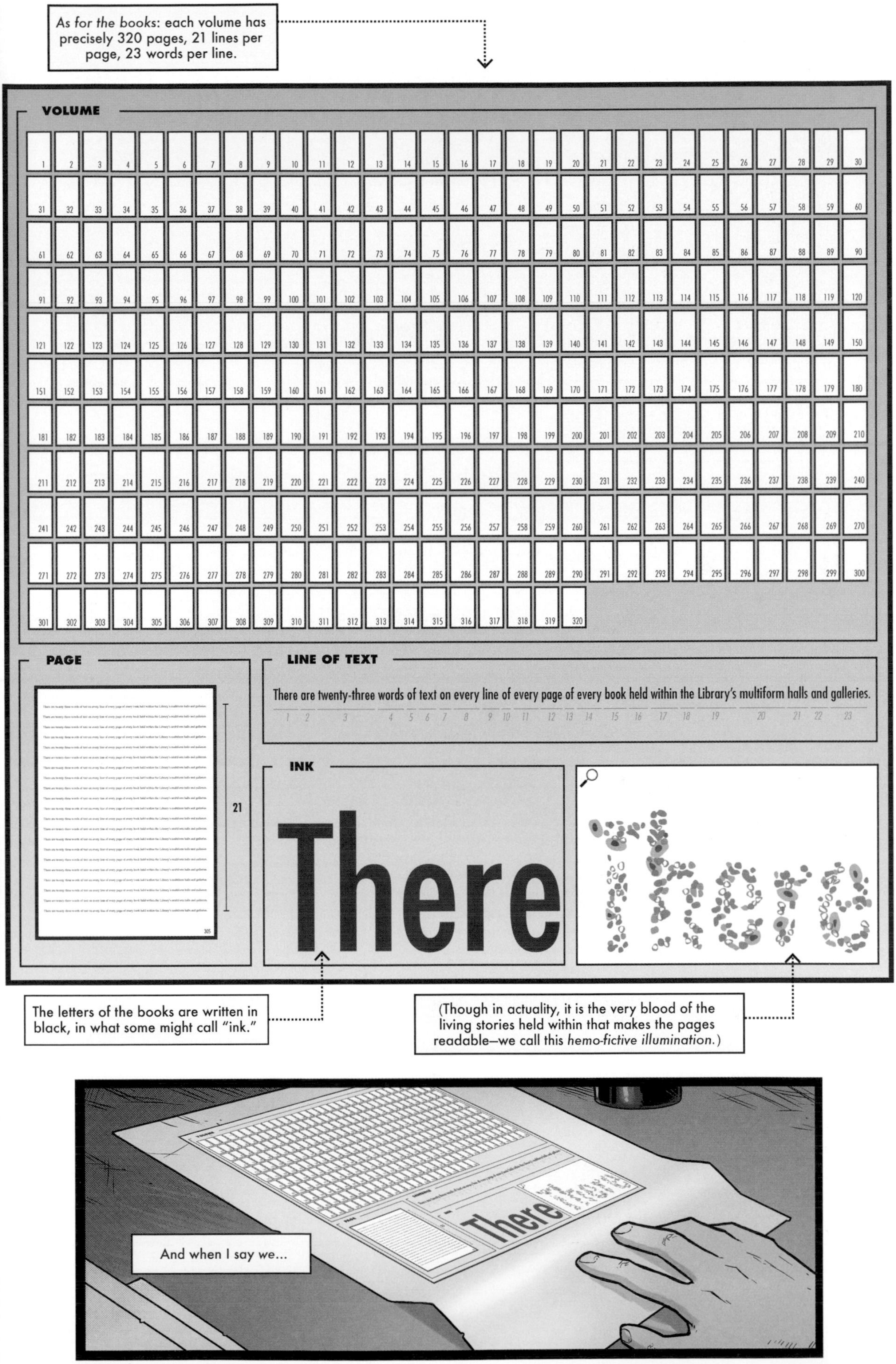
As for the books: each volume has precisely 320 pages, 21 lines per page, 23 words per line.
VOLUME
1 2 3 4 5 6 7 8 9 10 11 12 13 14 15 16 17 18 19 20 21 22 23 24 25 26 27 28 29 30
31 32 33 34 35 36 37 38 39 40 41 42 43 44 45 46 47 48 49 50 51 52 53 54 55 56 57 58 59 60
61 62 63 64 65 66 67 68 69 70 71 72 73 74 75 76 77 78 79 80 81 82 83 84 85 86 87 88 89 90
91 92 93 94 95 96 97 98 99 100 101 102 103 104 105 106 107 108 109 110 111 112 113 114 115 116 117 118 119 120
121 122 123 124 125 126 127 128 129 130 131 132 133 134 135 136 137 138 139 140 141 142 143 144 145 146 147 148 149 150
151 152 153 154 155 156 157 158 159 160 161 162 163 164 165 166 167 168 169 170 171 172 173 174 175 176 177 178 179 180
181 182 183 184 185 186 187 188 189 190 191 192 193 194 195 196 197 198 199 200 201 202 203 204 205 206 207 208 209 210
211 212 213 214 215 216 217 218 219 220 221 222 223 224 225 226 227 228 229 230 231 232 233 234 235 236 237 238 239 240
241 242 243 244 245 246 247 248 249 250 251 252 253 254 255 256 257 258 259 260 261 262 263 264 265 266 267 268 269 270
271 272 273 274 275 276 277 278 279 280 281 282 283 284 285 286 287 288 289 290 291 292 293 294 295 296 297 298 299 300
301 302 303 304 305 306 307 308 309 310 311 312 313 314 315 316 317 318 319 320
PAGE
21
305
LINE OF TEXT
There are twenty-three words of text on every line of every page of every book held within the Library's multiform halls and galleries.
1 2 3 4 5 6 7 8 9 10 11 12 13 14 15 16 17 18 19 20 21 22 23
INK
There
There
The letters of the books are written in black, in what some might call "ink."
(Though in actuality, it is the very blood of the living stories held within that makes the pages readable—we call this *hemo-fictive illumination.*)
And when I say we...

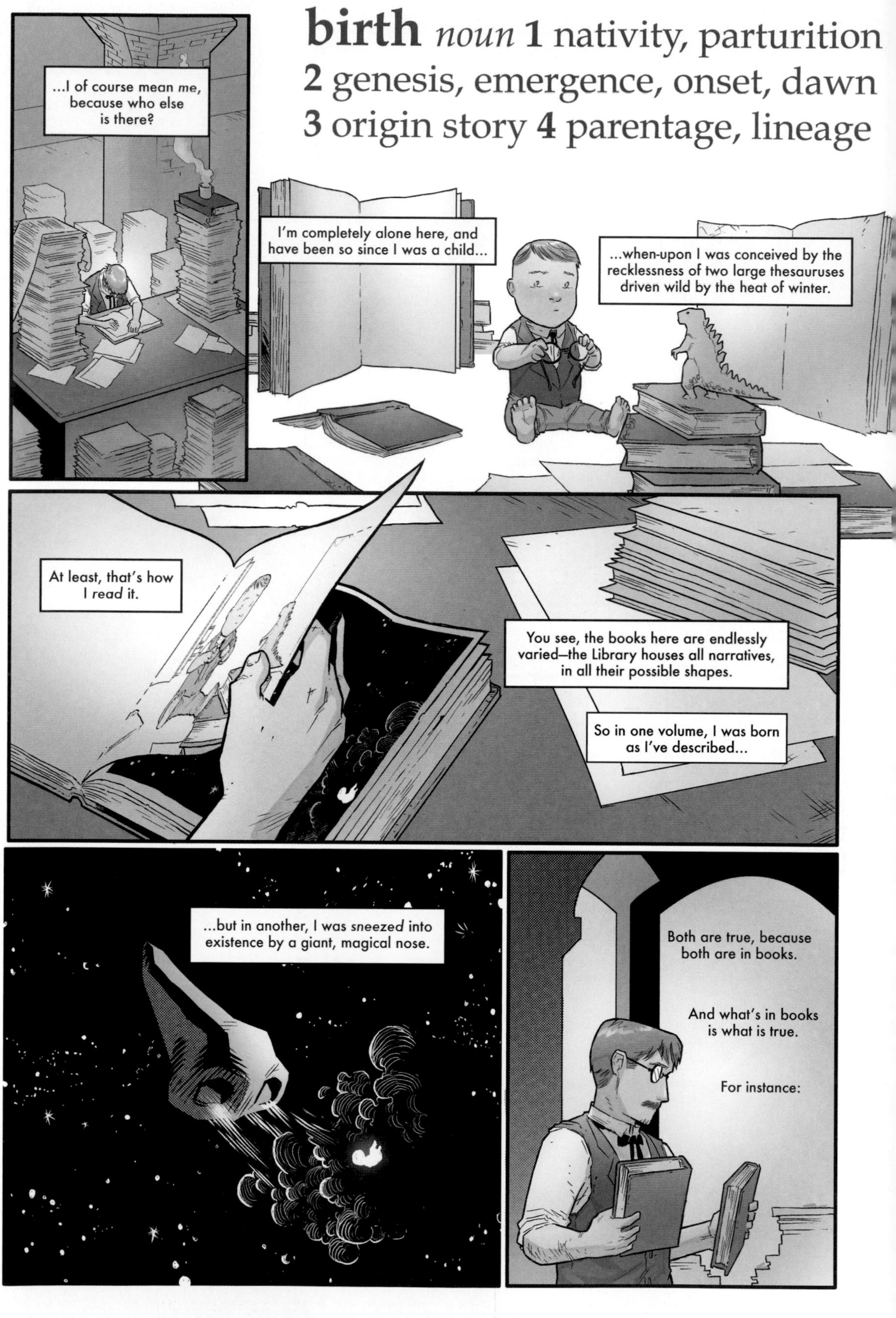

birth *noun* 1 nativity, parturition 2 genesis, emergence, onset, dawn 3 origin story 4 parentage, lineage
...I of course mean *me*, because who else is there?
I'm completely alone here, and have been so since I was a child...
...when-upon I was conceived by the recklessness of two large thesauruses driven wild by the heat of winter.
At least, that's how I *read* it.
You see, the books here are endlessly varied—the Library houses all narratives, in all their possible shapes.
So in one volume, I was born as I've described...
...but in another, I was *sneezed* into existence by a giant, magical nose.
Both are true, because both are in books.
And what's in books is what is true.
For instance:

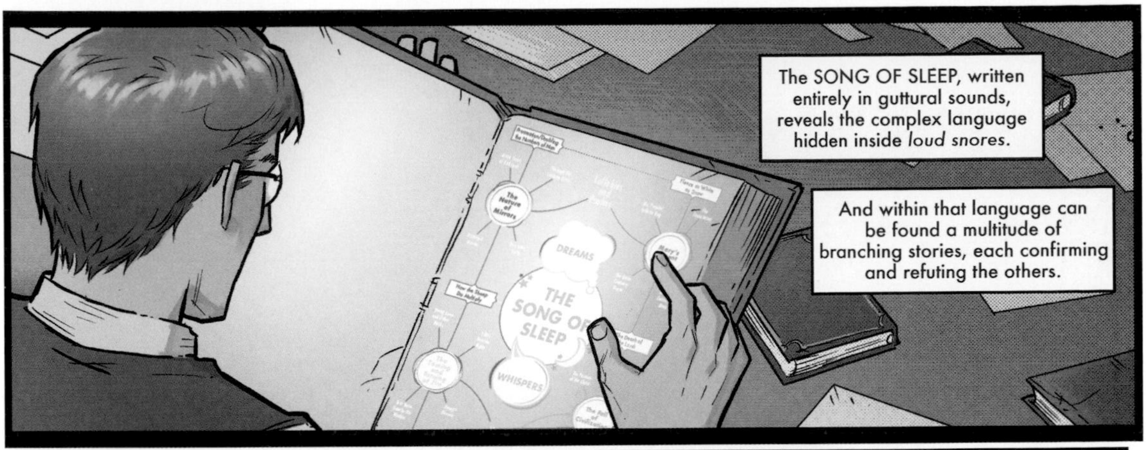

The SONG OF SLEEP, written entirely in guttural sounds, reveals the complex language hidden inside *loud snores*.
And within that language can be found a multitude of branching stories, each confirming and refuting the others.

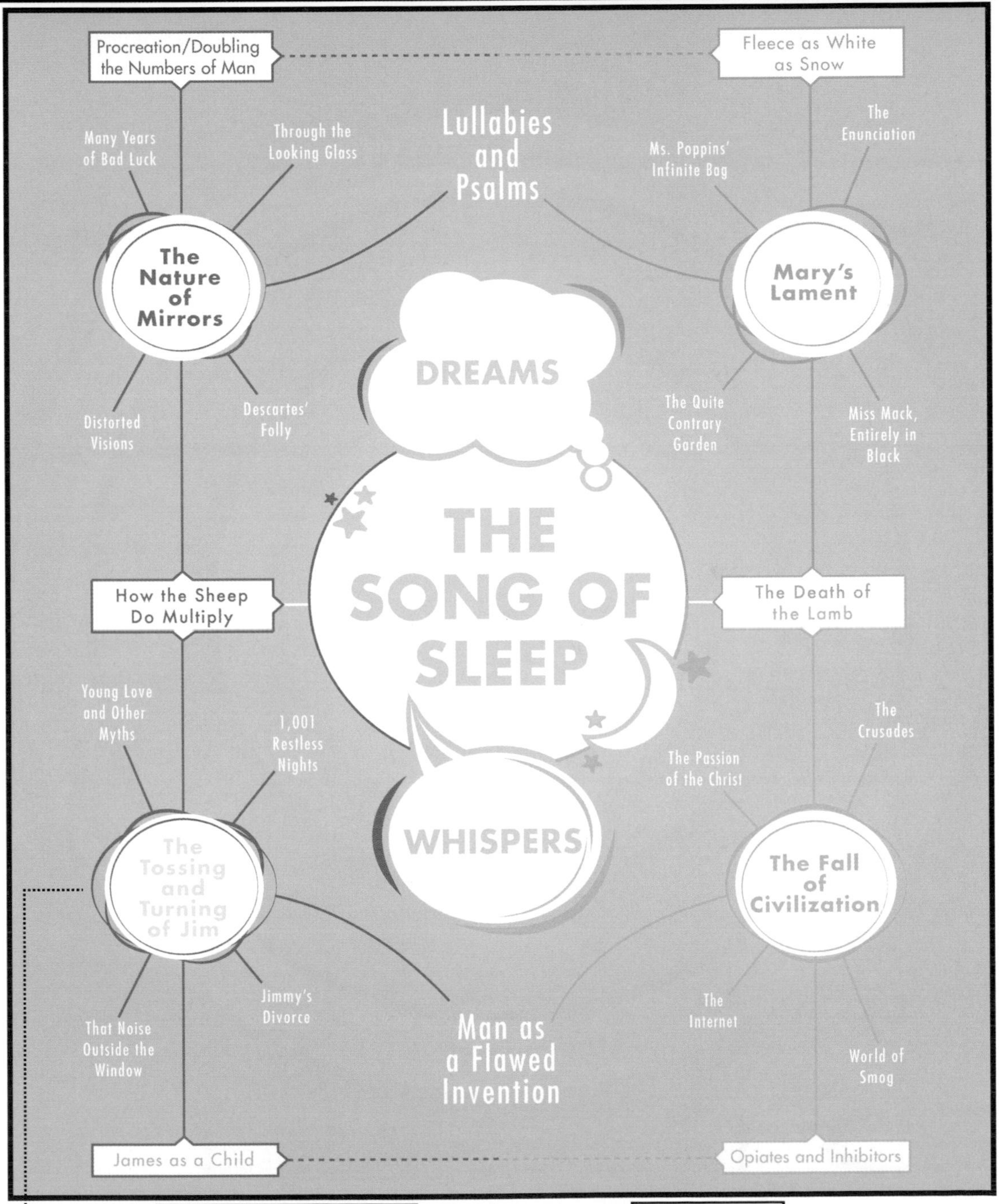

Procreation/Doubling the Numbers of Man
Fleece as White as Snow
Many Years of Bad Luck
Through the Looking Glass
Lullabies and Psalms
Ms. Poppins' Infinite Bag
The Enunciation
The Nature of Mirrors
Mary's Lament
DREAMS
Distorted Visions
Descartes' Folly
The Quite Contrary Garden
Miss Mack, Entirely in Black
THE SONG OF SLEEP
How the Sheep Do Multiply
The Death of the Lamb
Young Love and Other Myths
1,001 Restless Nights
The Crusades
The Passion of the Christ
WHISPERS
The Tossing and Turning of Jim
The Fall of Civilization
Jimmy's Divorce
That Noise Outside the Window
Man as a Flawed Invention
The Internet
World of Smog
James as a Child
Opiates and Inhibitors

It goes on forever, if you're interested enough to read it all.

My point being:

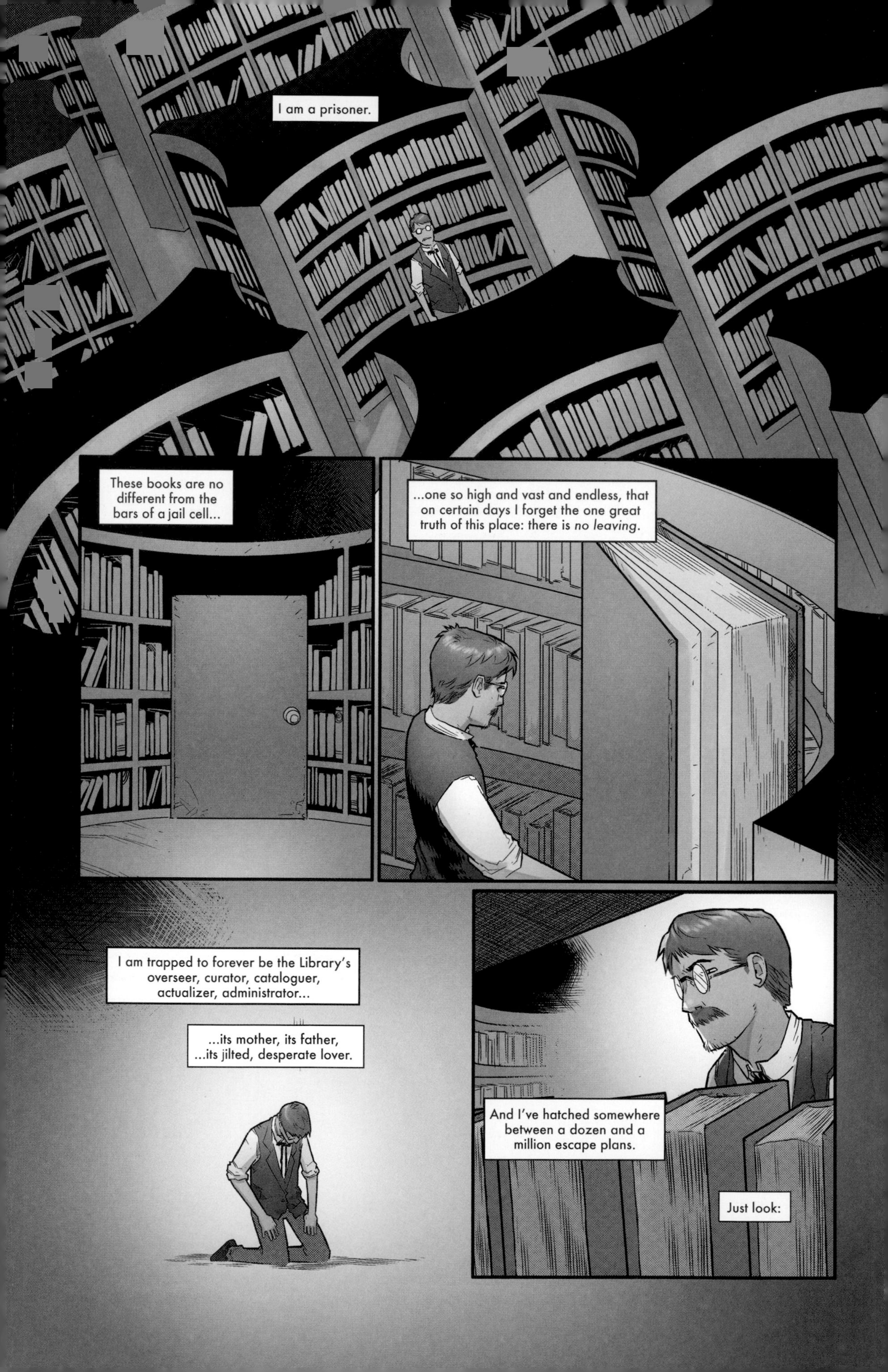
I am a prisoner.
These books are no different from the bars of a jail cell...
...one so high and vast and endless, that on certain days I forget the one great truth of this place: there is *no leaving*.
I am trapped to forever be the Library's overseer, curator, cataloguer, actualizer, administrator...
...its mother, its father, ...its jilted, desperate lover.
And I've hatched somewhere between a dozen and a million escape plans.
Just look:

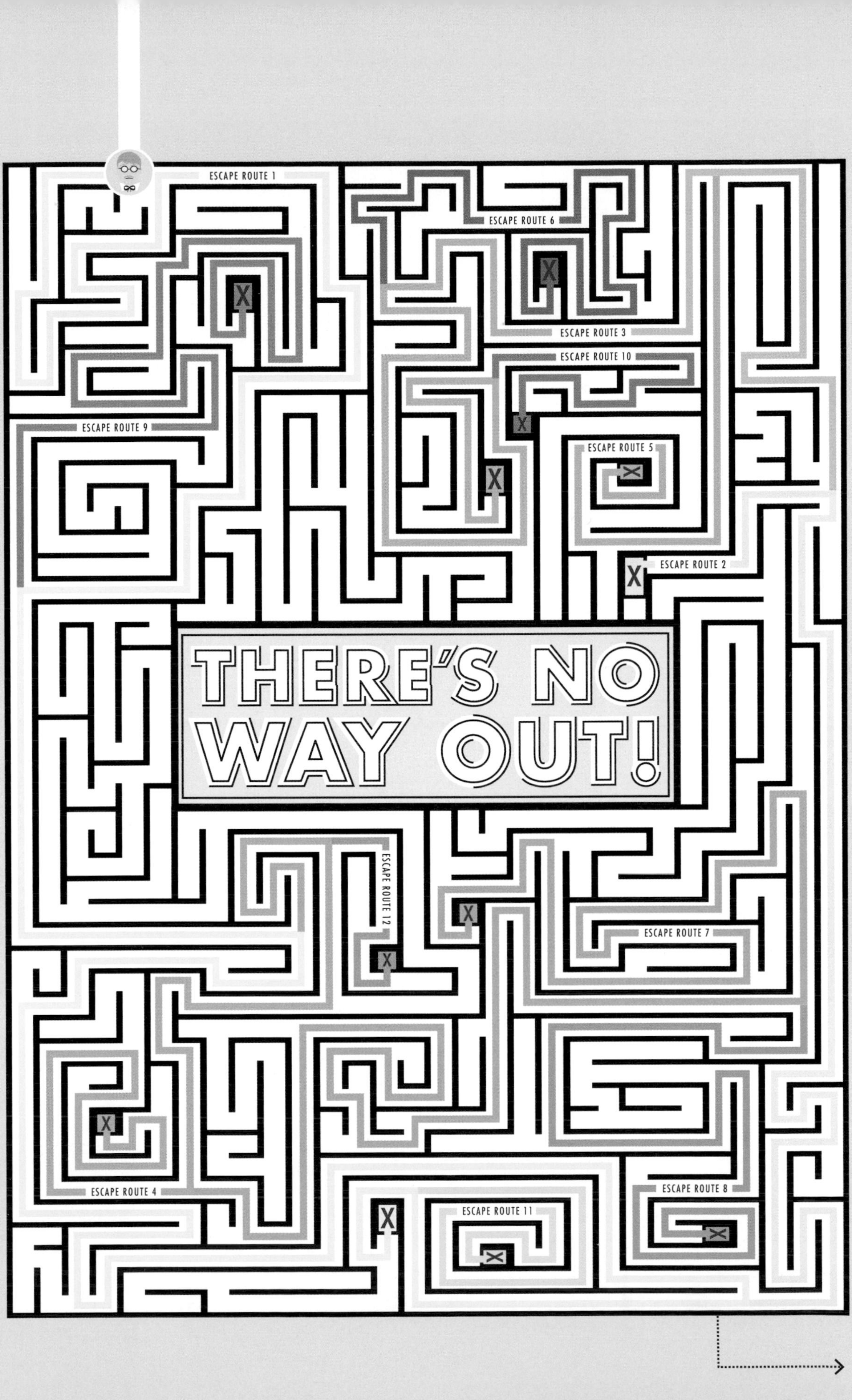

ESCAPE ROUTE 1
ESCAPE ROUTE 6
ESCAPE ROUTE 3
ESCAPE ROUTE 10
ESCAPE ROUTE 9
ESCAPE ROUTE 5
ESCAPE ROUTE 2
THERE'S NO WAY OUT!
ESCAPE ROUTE 12
ESCAPE ROUTE 7
ESCAPE ROUTE 4
ESCAPE ROUTE 8
ESCAPE ROUTE 11

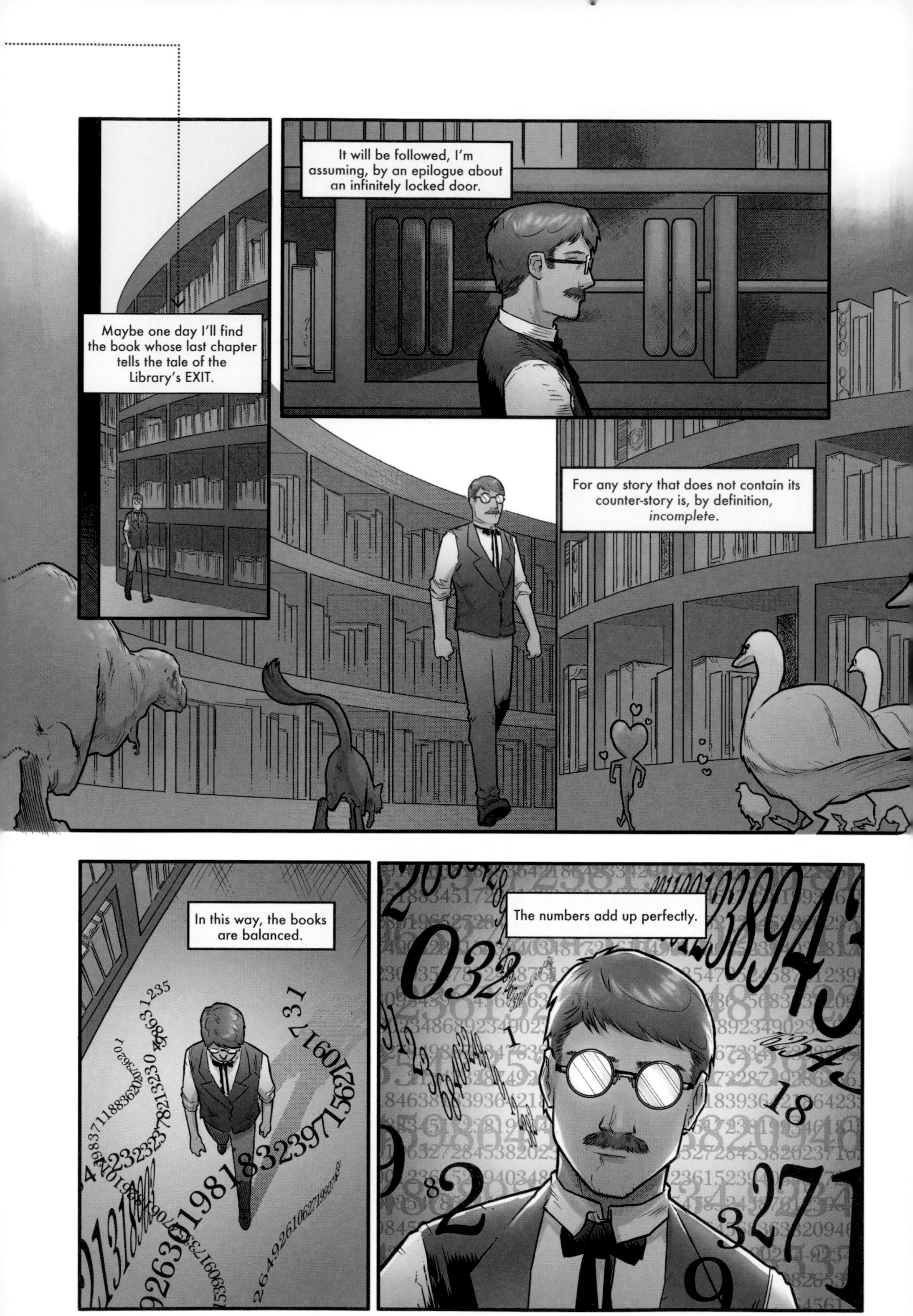
Maybe one day I'll find the book whose last chapter tells the tale of the Library's EXIT.
It will be followed, I'm assuming, by an epilogue about an infinitely locked door.
For any story that does not contain its counter-story is, by definition, *incomplete*.
In this way, the books are balanced.
The numbers add up perfectly.

The End

MONDAY

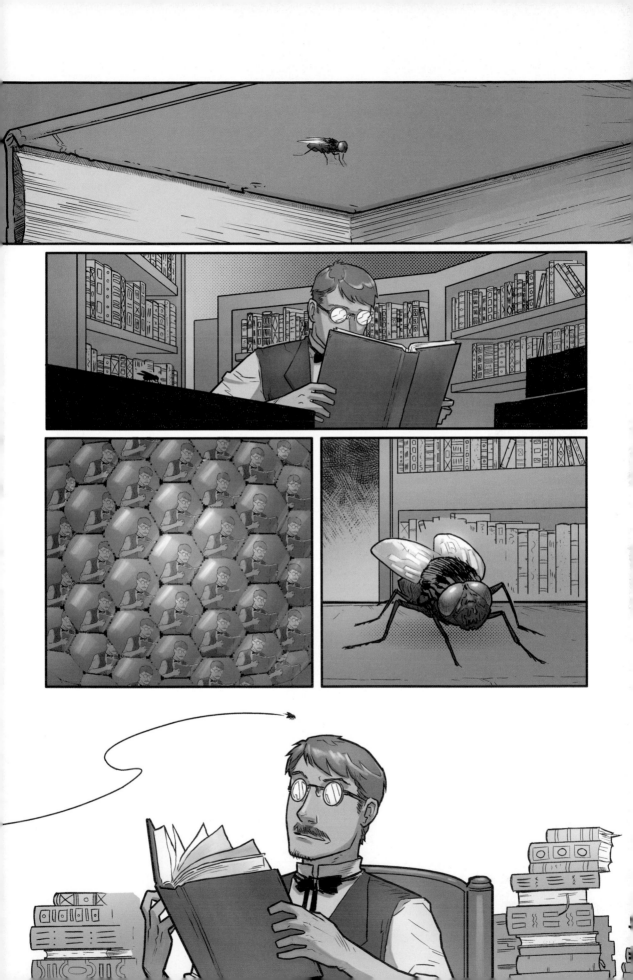

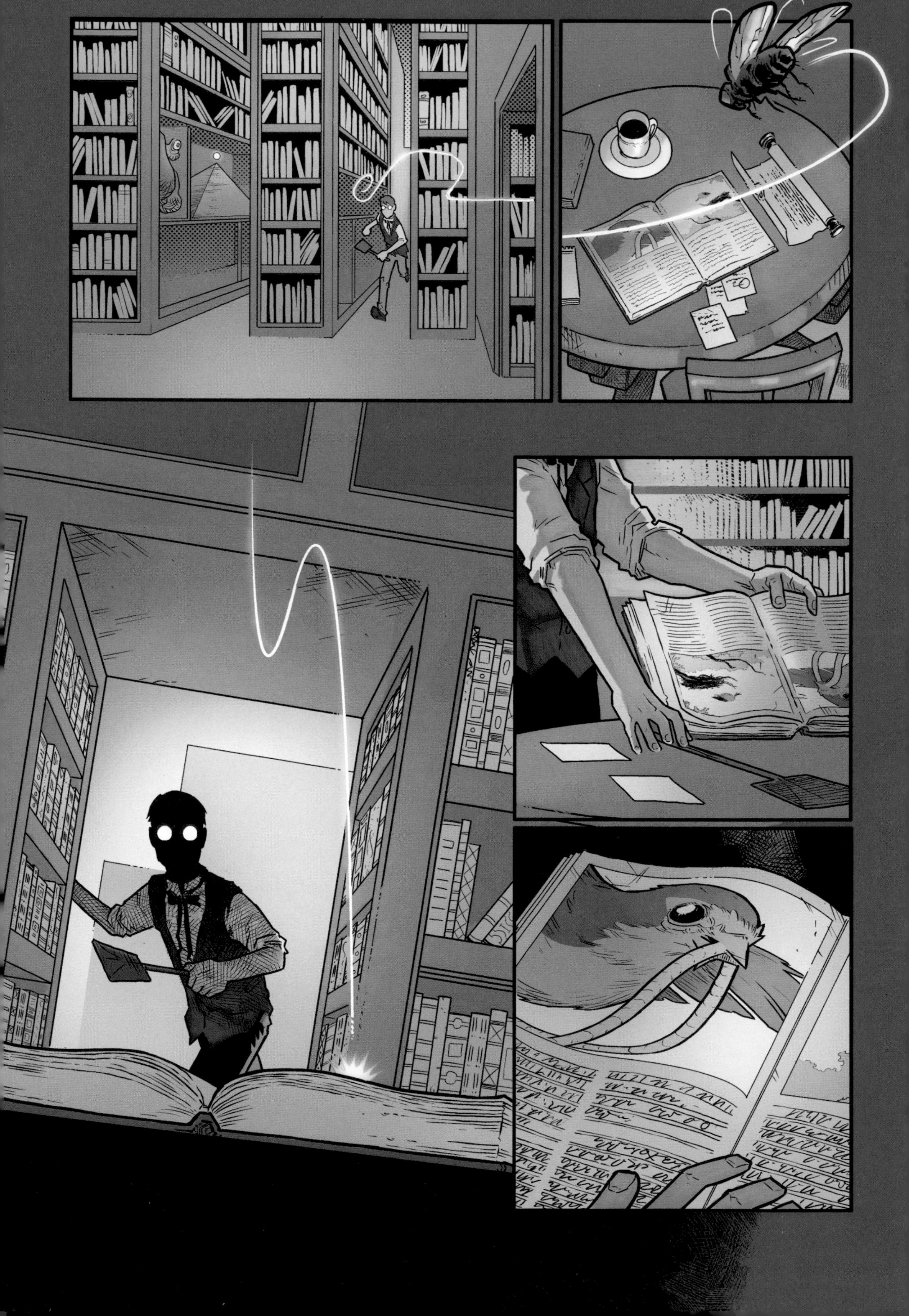

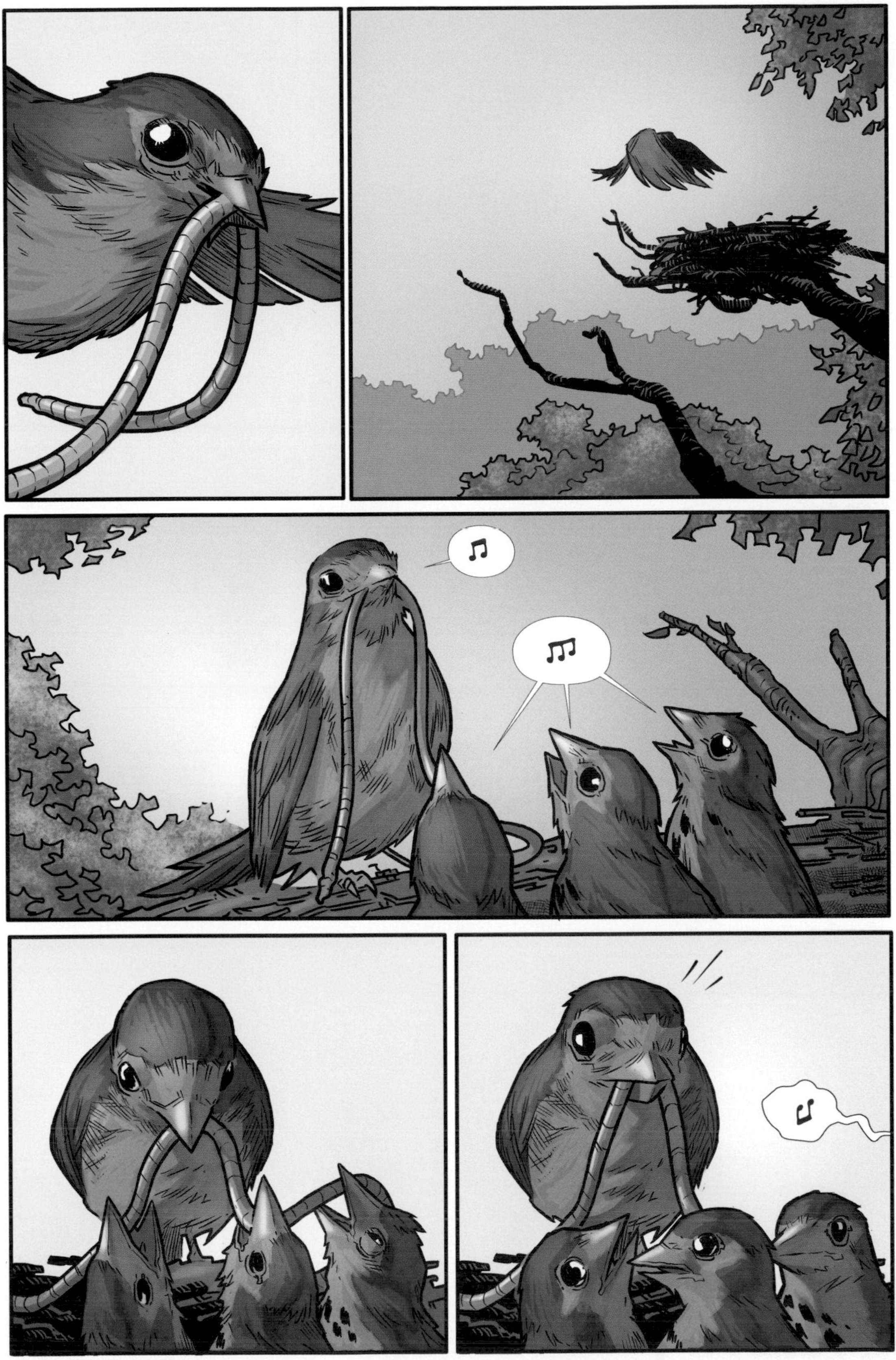

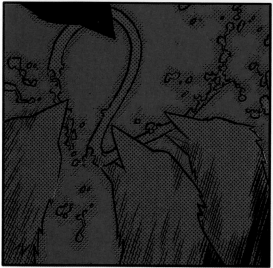

*Translated from Birdese

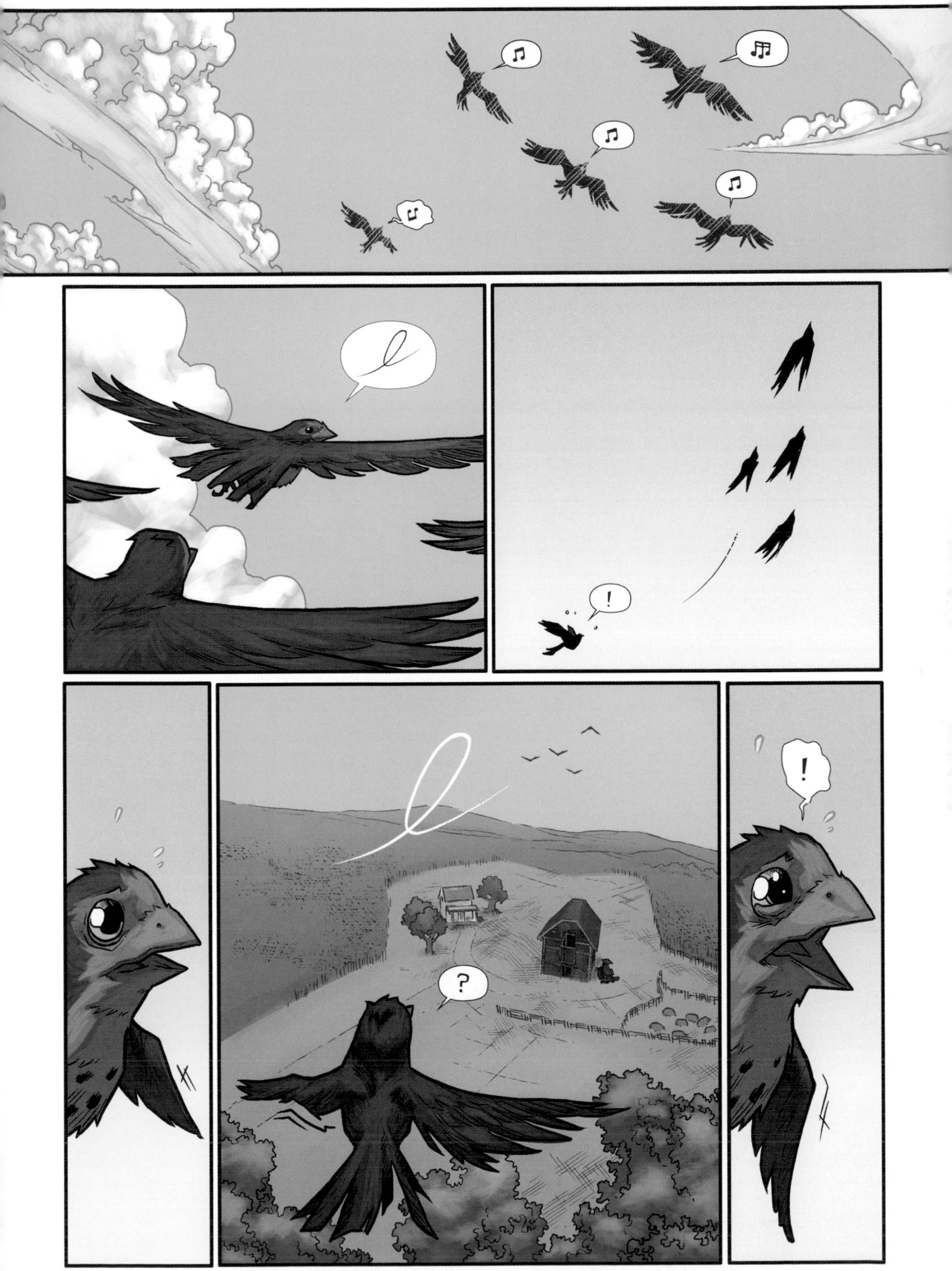
!
?
!

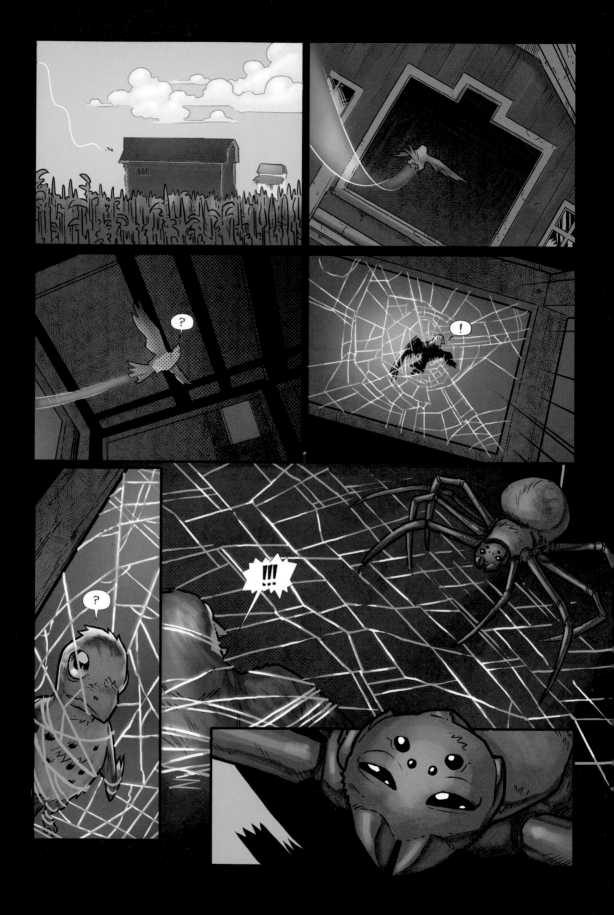

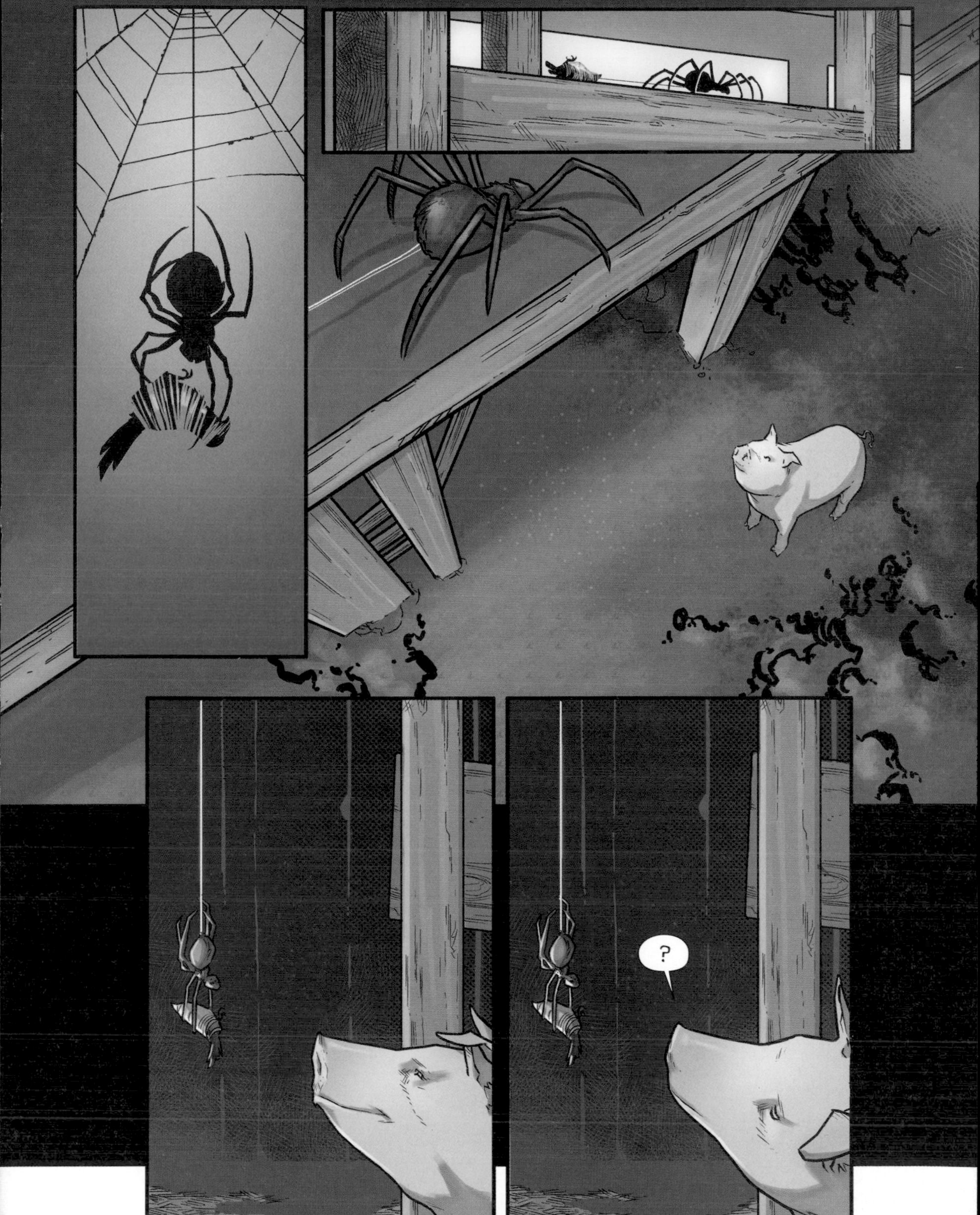
?

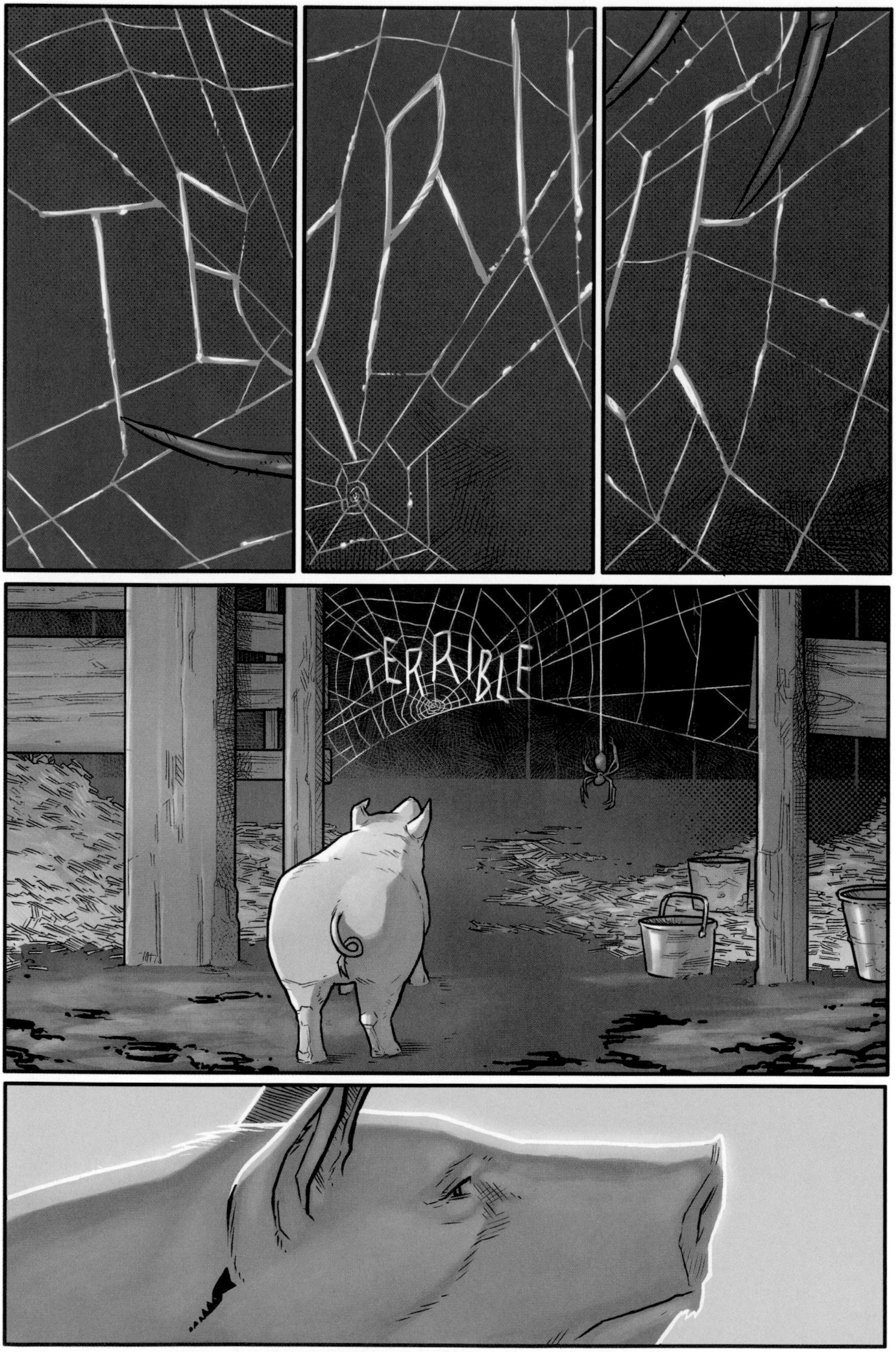
TERRIBLE

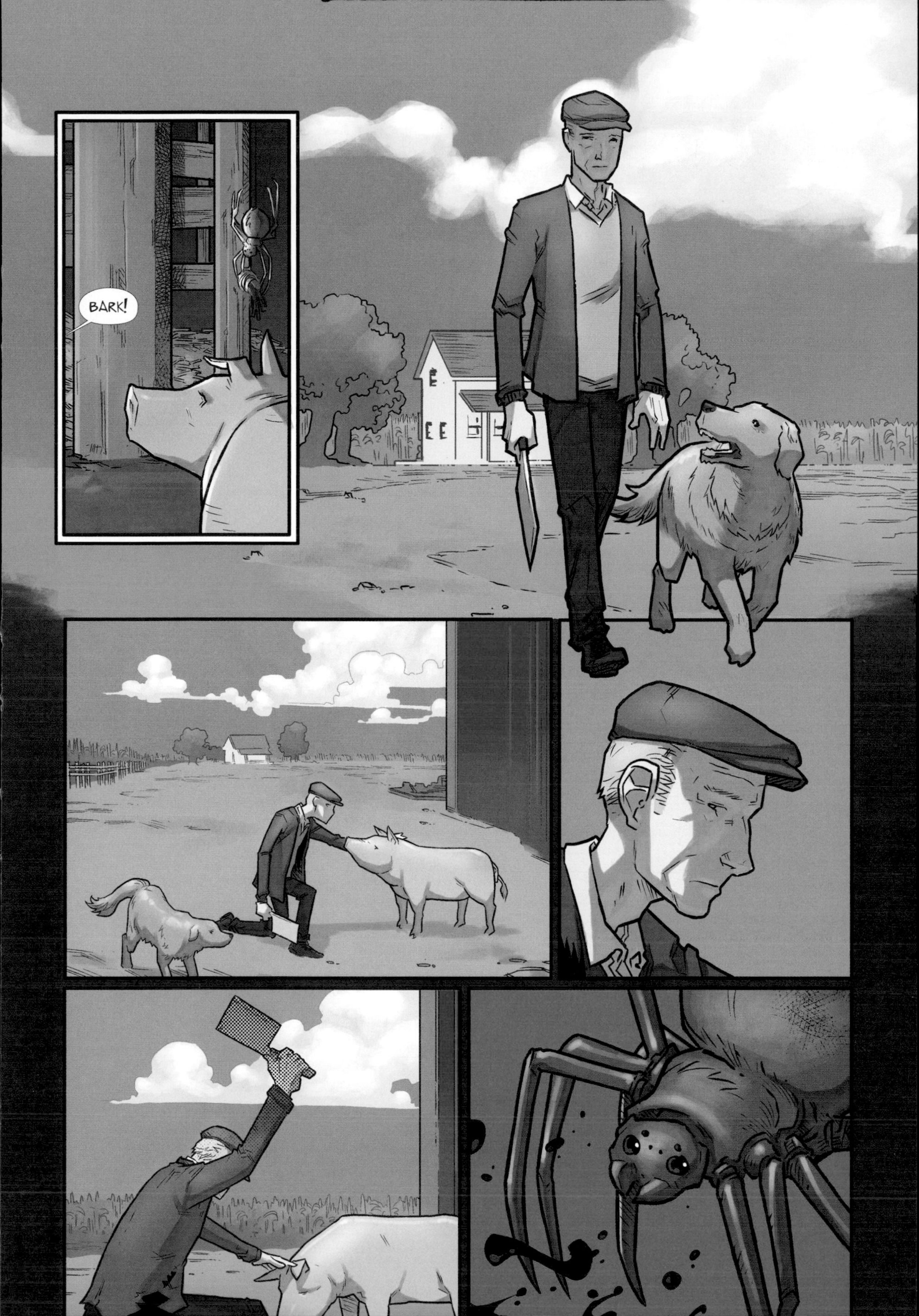
BARK!

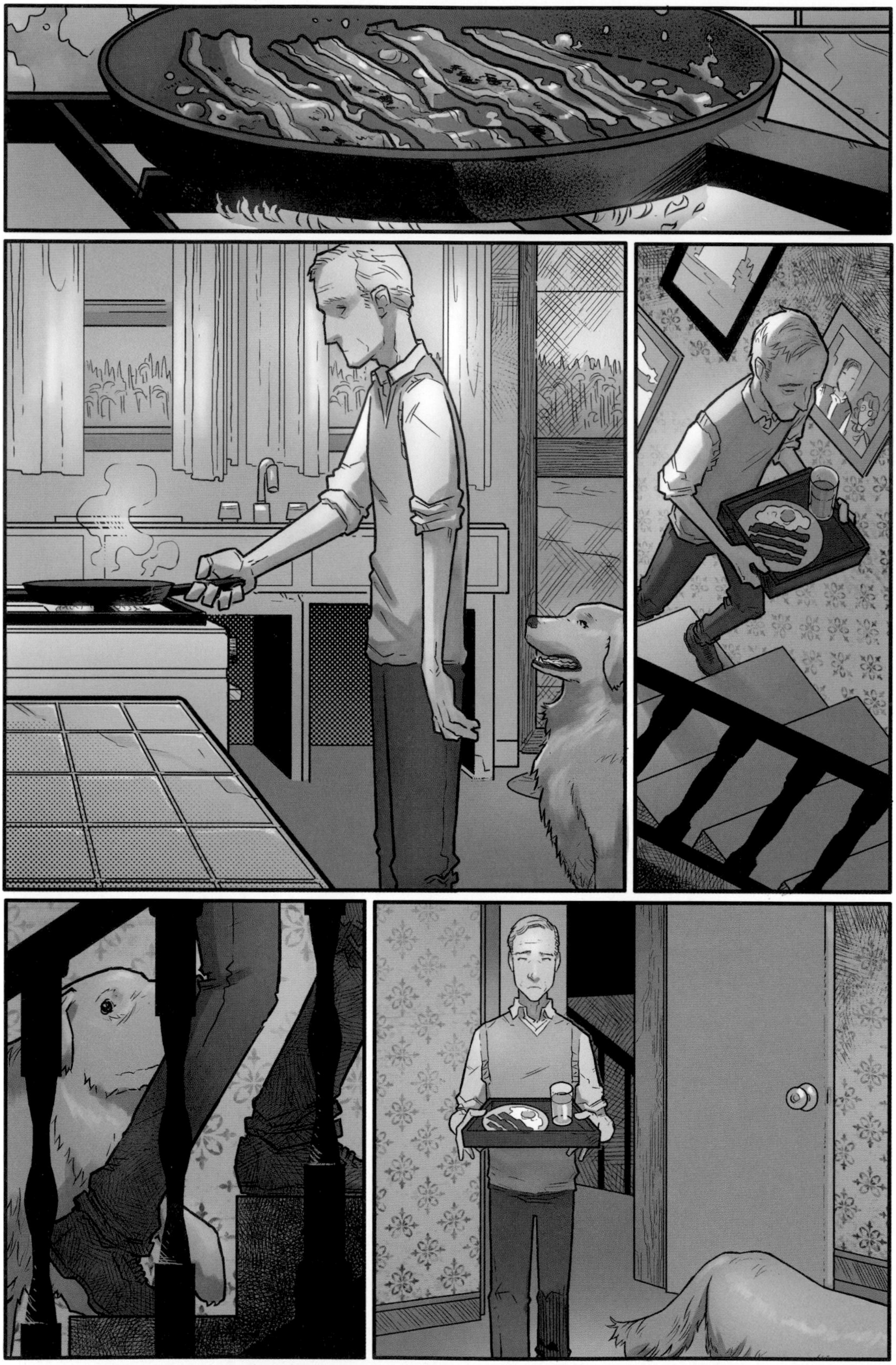

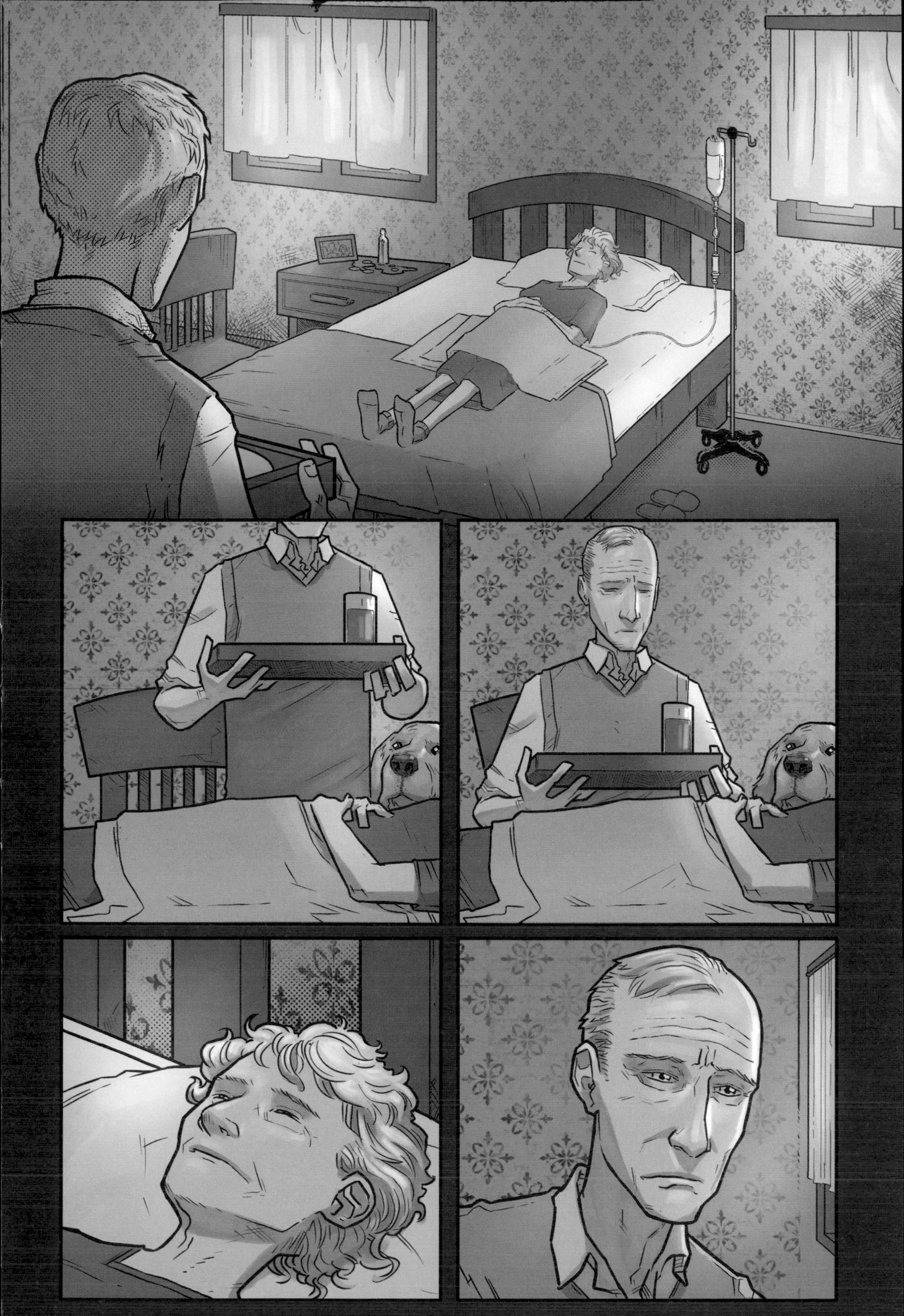

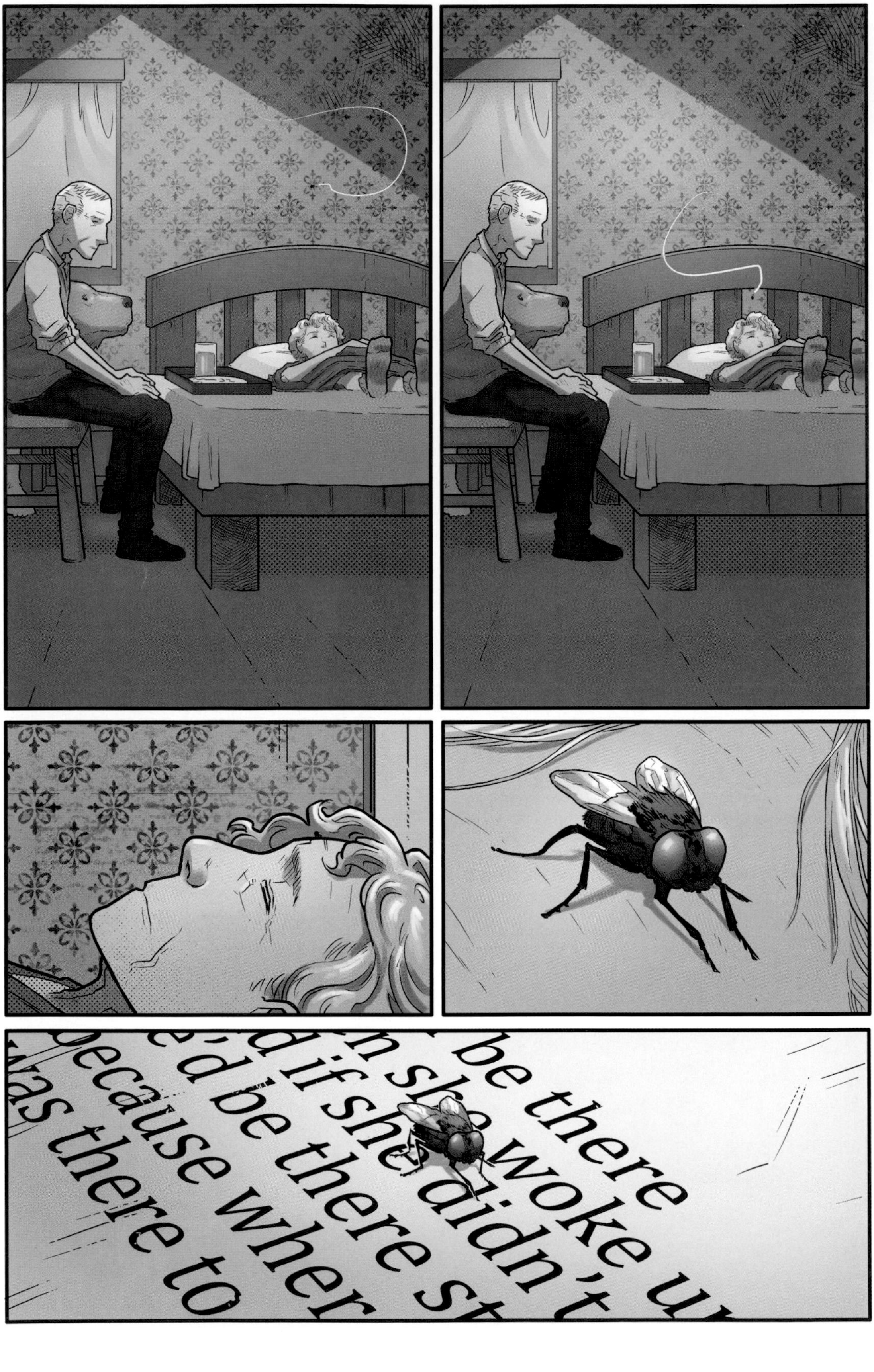
be there
she woke
if she didn't
be there
because
there to

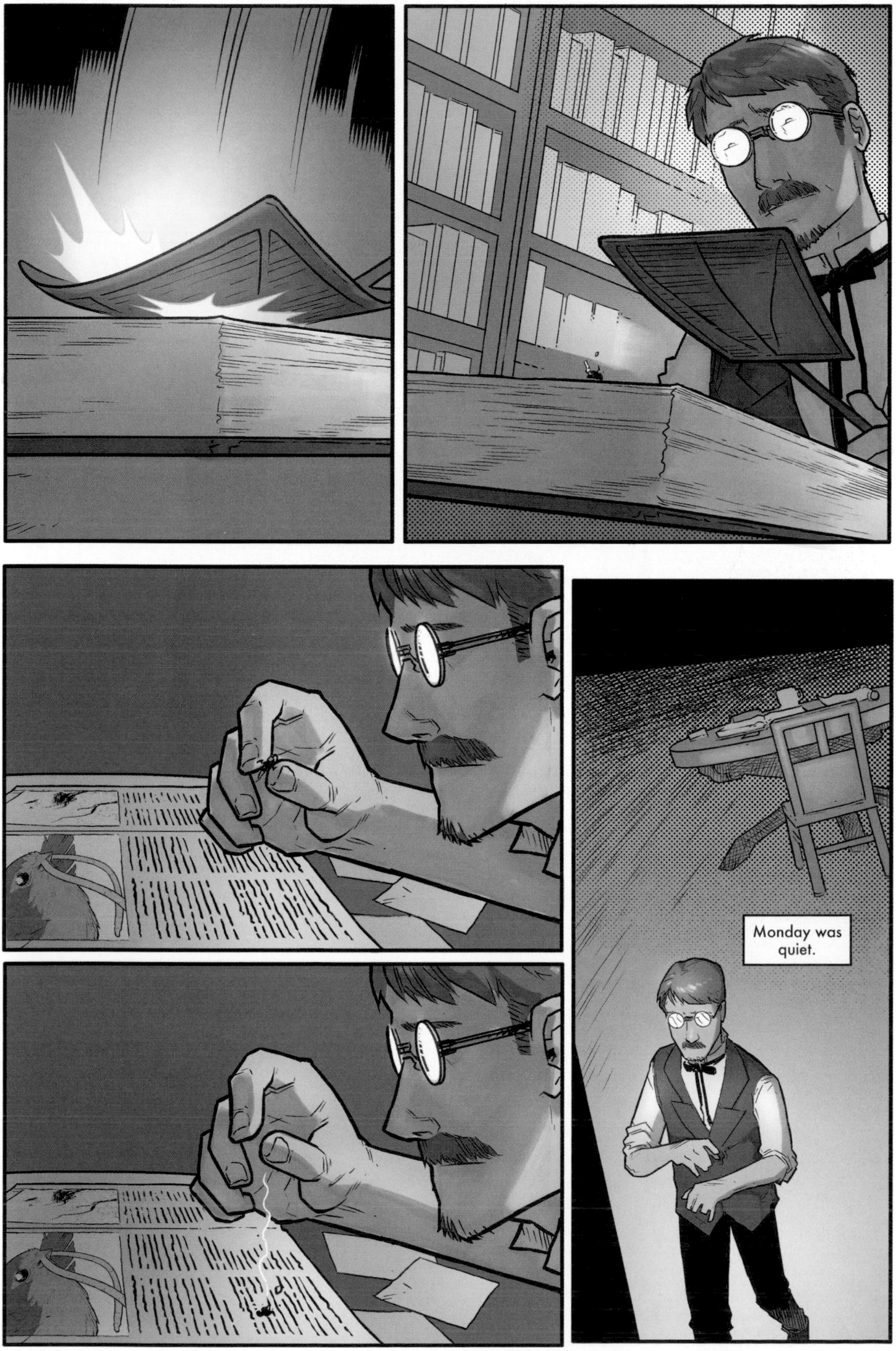
Monday was quiet.

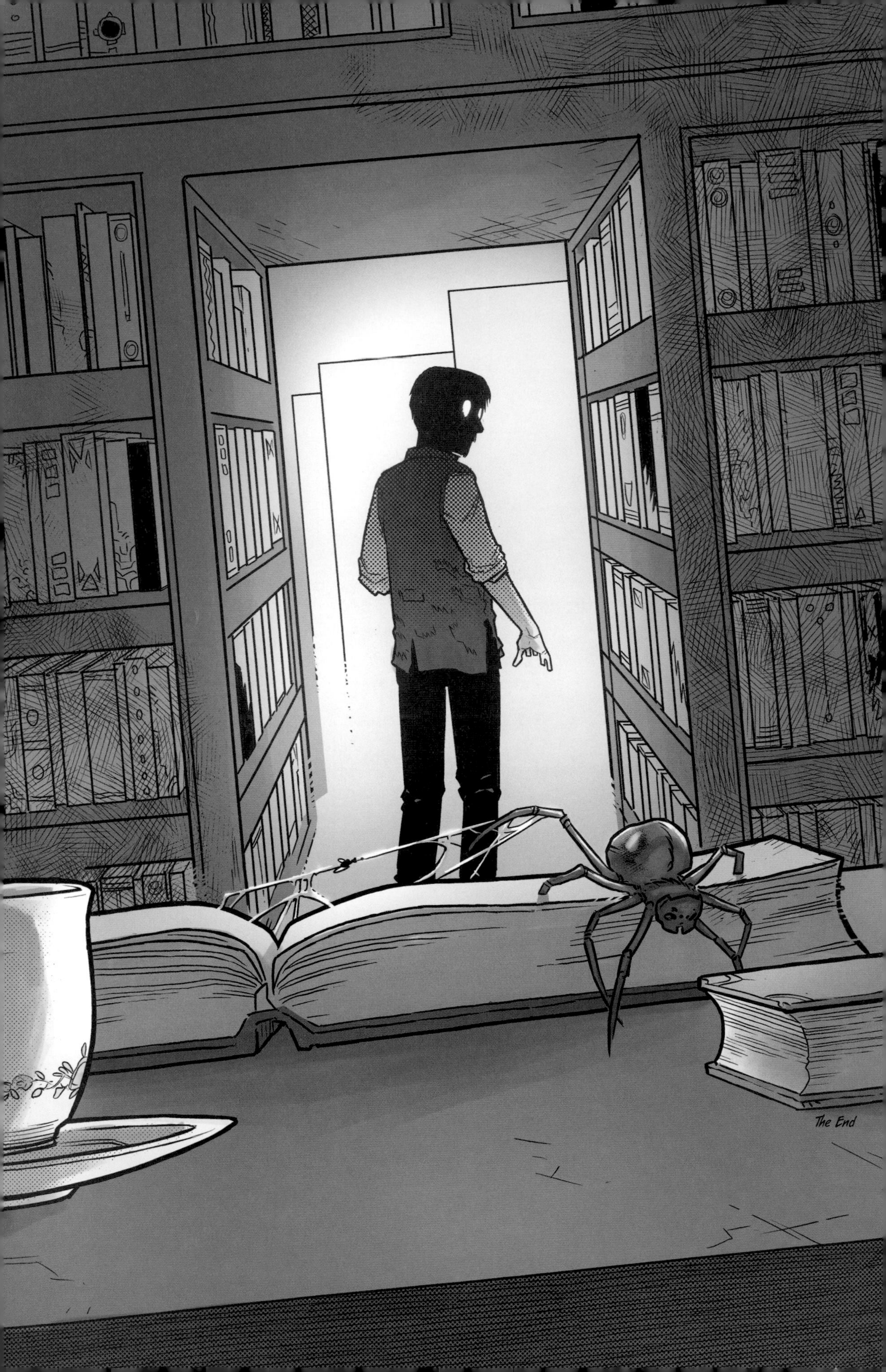
The End

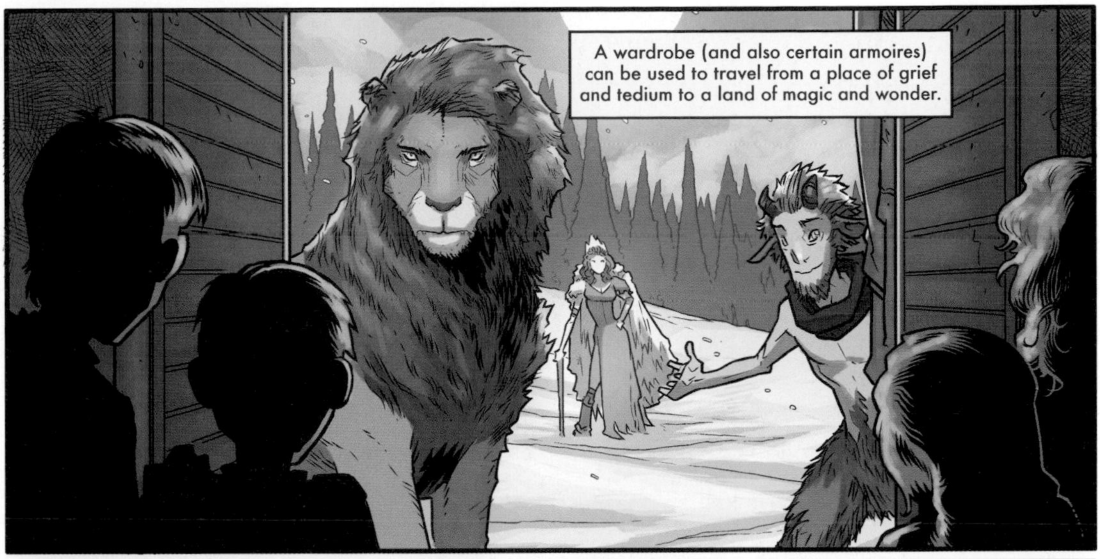
A wardrobe (and also certain armoires) can be used to travel from a place of grief and tedium to a land of magic and wonder.

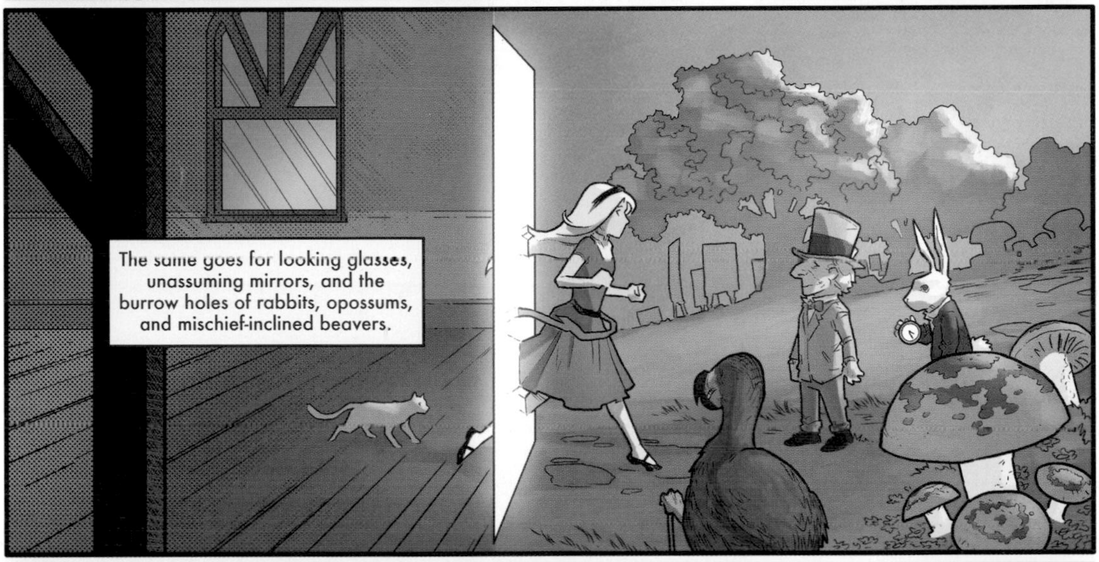
The same goes for looking glasses, unassuming mirrors, and the burrow holes of rabbits, opossums, and mischief-inclined beavers.

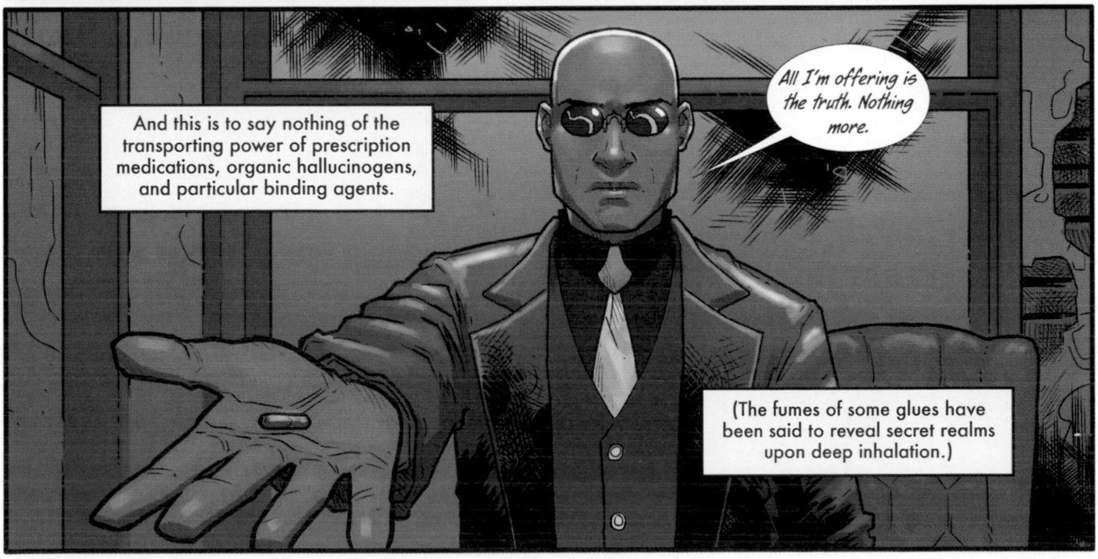
And this is to say nothing of the transporting power of prescription medications, organic hallucinogens, and particular binding agents.
All I'm offering is the truth. Nothing more.
(The fumes of some glues have been said to reveal secret realms upon deep inhalation.)

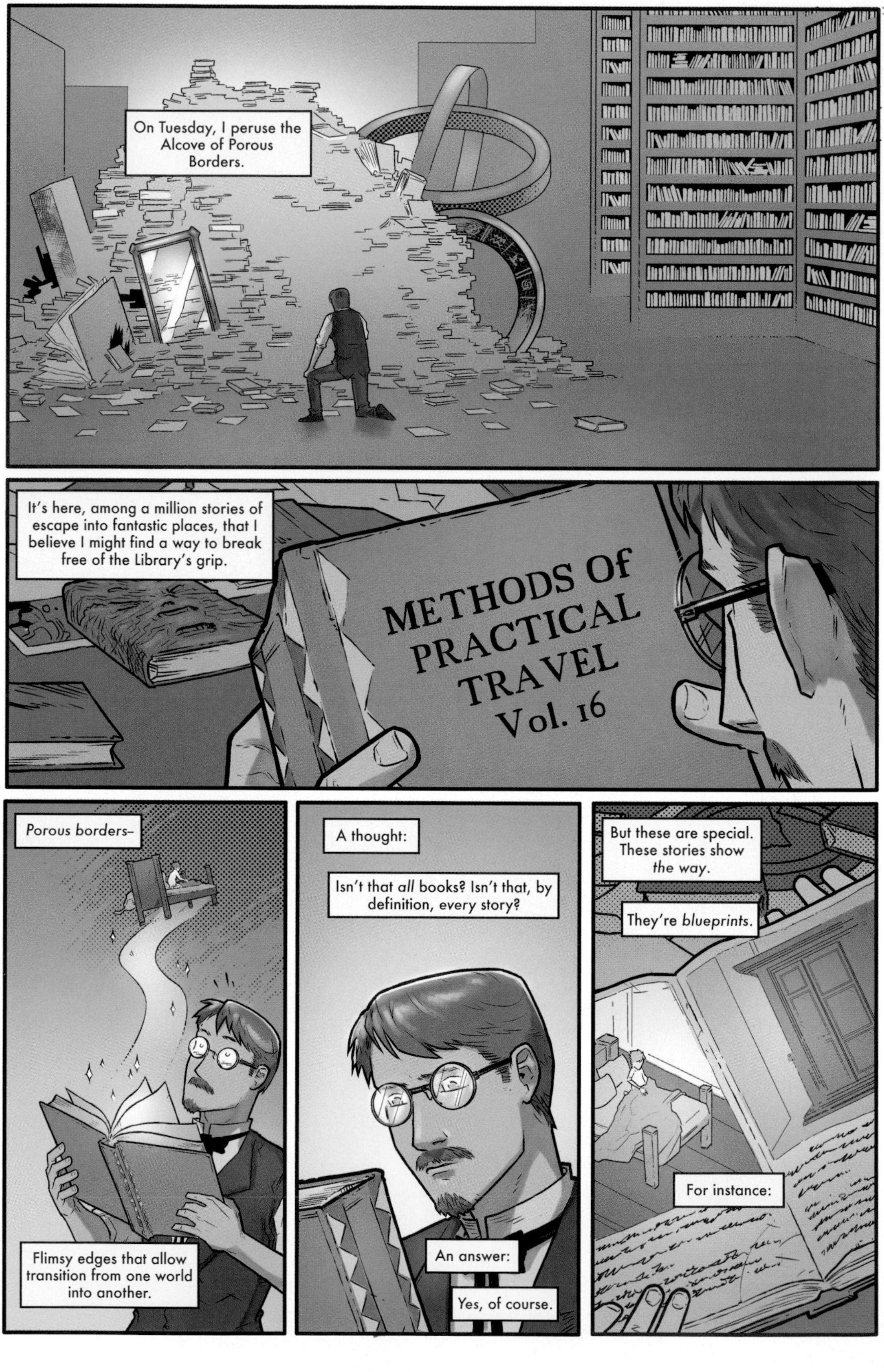
On Tuesday, I peruse the Alcove of Porous Borders.
It's here, among a million stories of escape into fantastic places, that I believe I might find a way to break free of the Library's grip.
METHODS OF PRACTICAL TRAVEL Vol. 16
Porous borders–
Flimsy edges that allow transition from one world into another.
A thought:
Isn't that *all* books? Isn't that, by definition, *every* story?
An answer:
Yes, of course.
But these are special. These stories show *the way.*
They're *blueprints.*
For instance:

TUESDAY

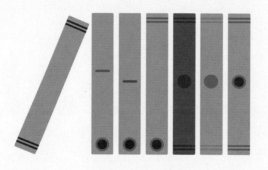

And then I see it.

A thing both strangely familiar and completely, utterly foreign.

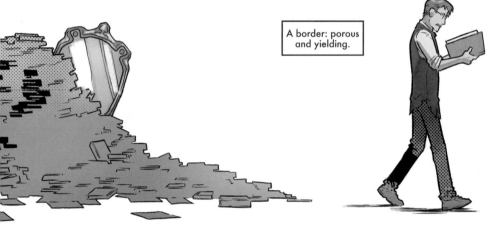

A border: porous and yielding.

A way out?

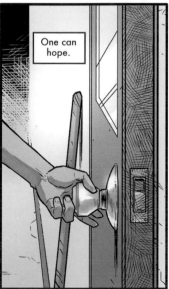

One can hope.

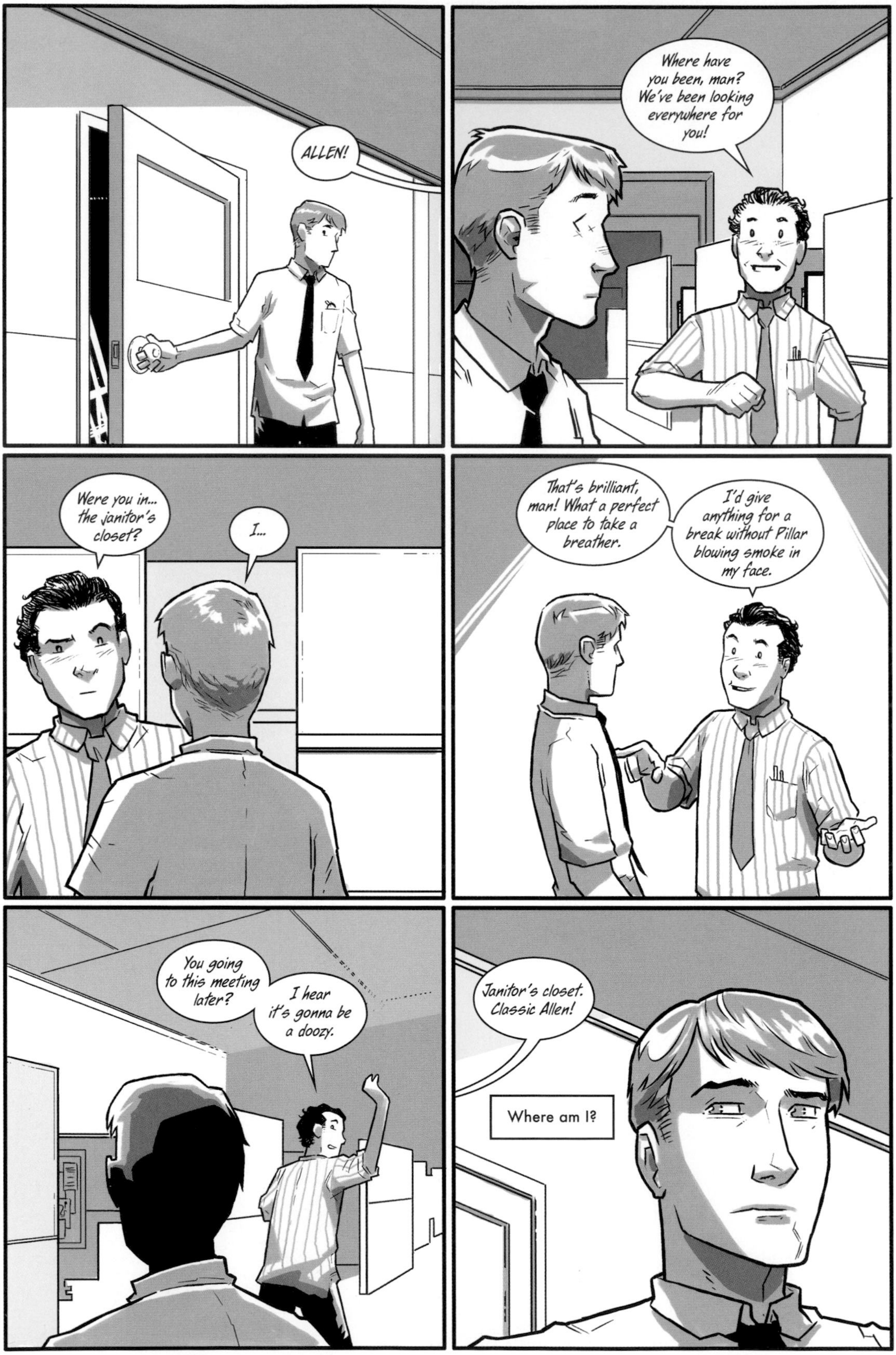
ALLEN!
Where have you been, man? We've been looking everywhere for you!
Were you in... the janitor's closet?
I...
That's brilliant, man! What a perfect place to take a breather.
I'd give anything for a break without Pillar blowing smoke in my face.
You going to this meeting later?
I hear it's gonna be a doozy.
Janitor's closet. Classic Allen!
Where am I?

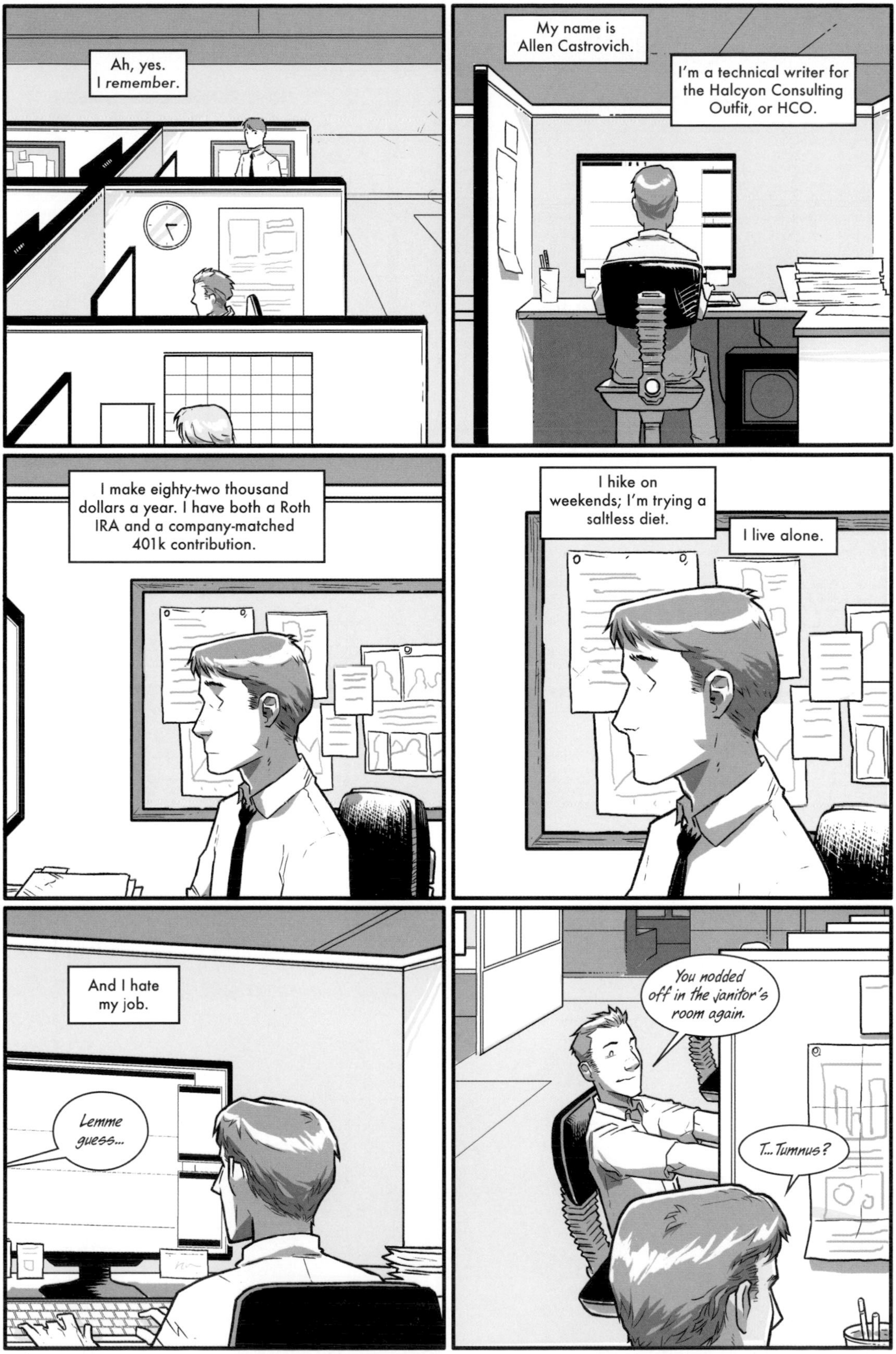
Ah, yes.
I remember.
My name is
Allen Castrovich.
I'm a technical writer for the Halcyon Consulting Outfit, or HCO.
I make eighty-two thousand dollars a year. I have both a Roth IRA and a company-matched 401k contribution.
I hike on weekends; I'm trying a saltless diet.
I live alone.
And I hate my job.
Lemme guess...
You nodded off in the janitor's room again.
T... Tumnus?

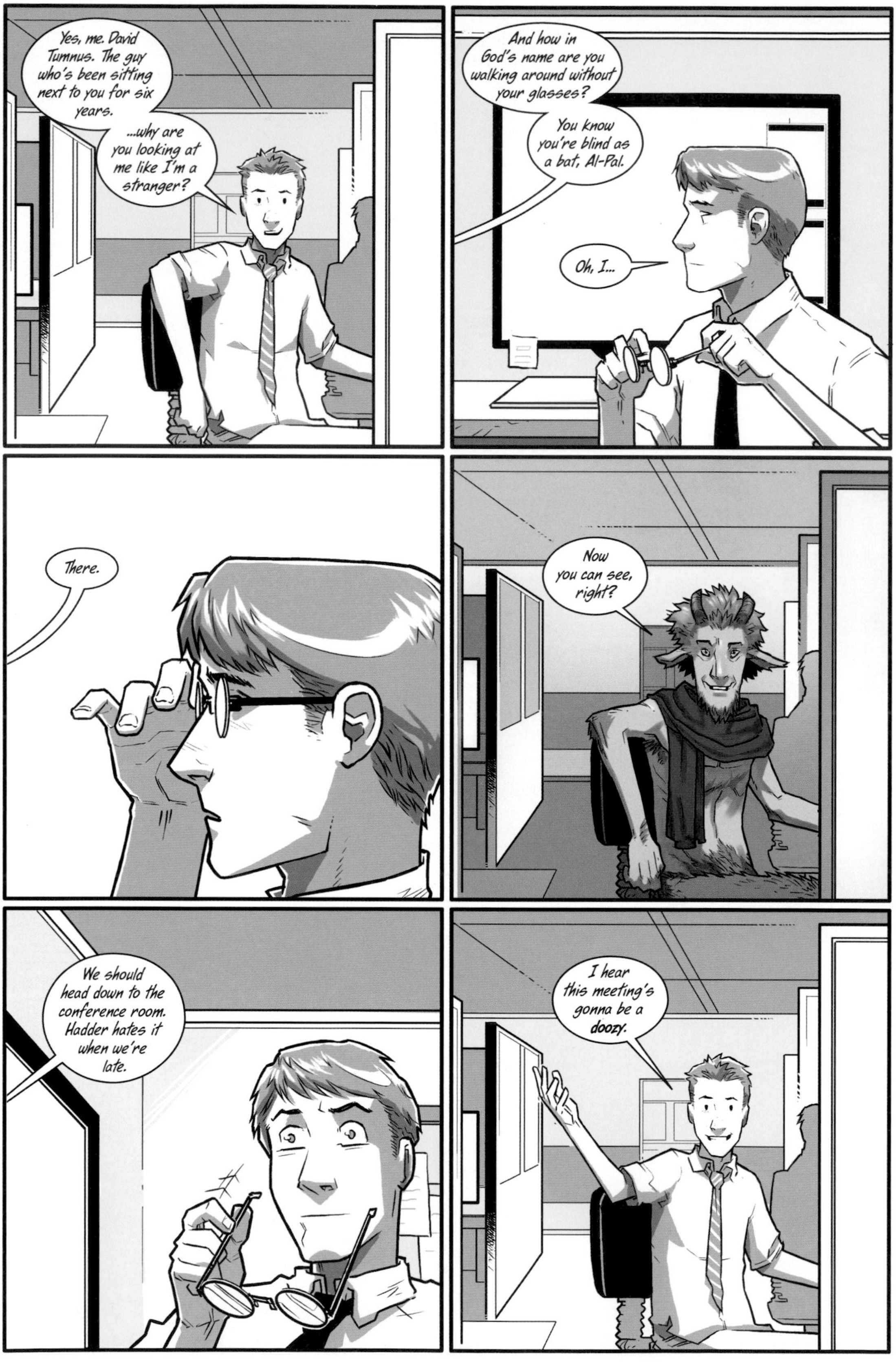
Yes, me. David Tumnus. The guy who's been sitting next to you for six years.
...why are you looking at me like I'm a stranger?
And how in God's name are you walking around without your glasses?
You know you're blind as a bat, Al-Pal.
Oh, I...
There.
Now you can see, right?
We should head down to the conference room. Hadder hates it when we're late.
I hear this meeting's gonna be a **doozy**.

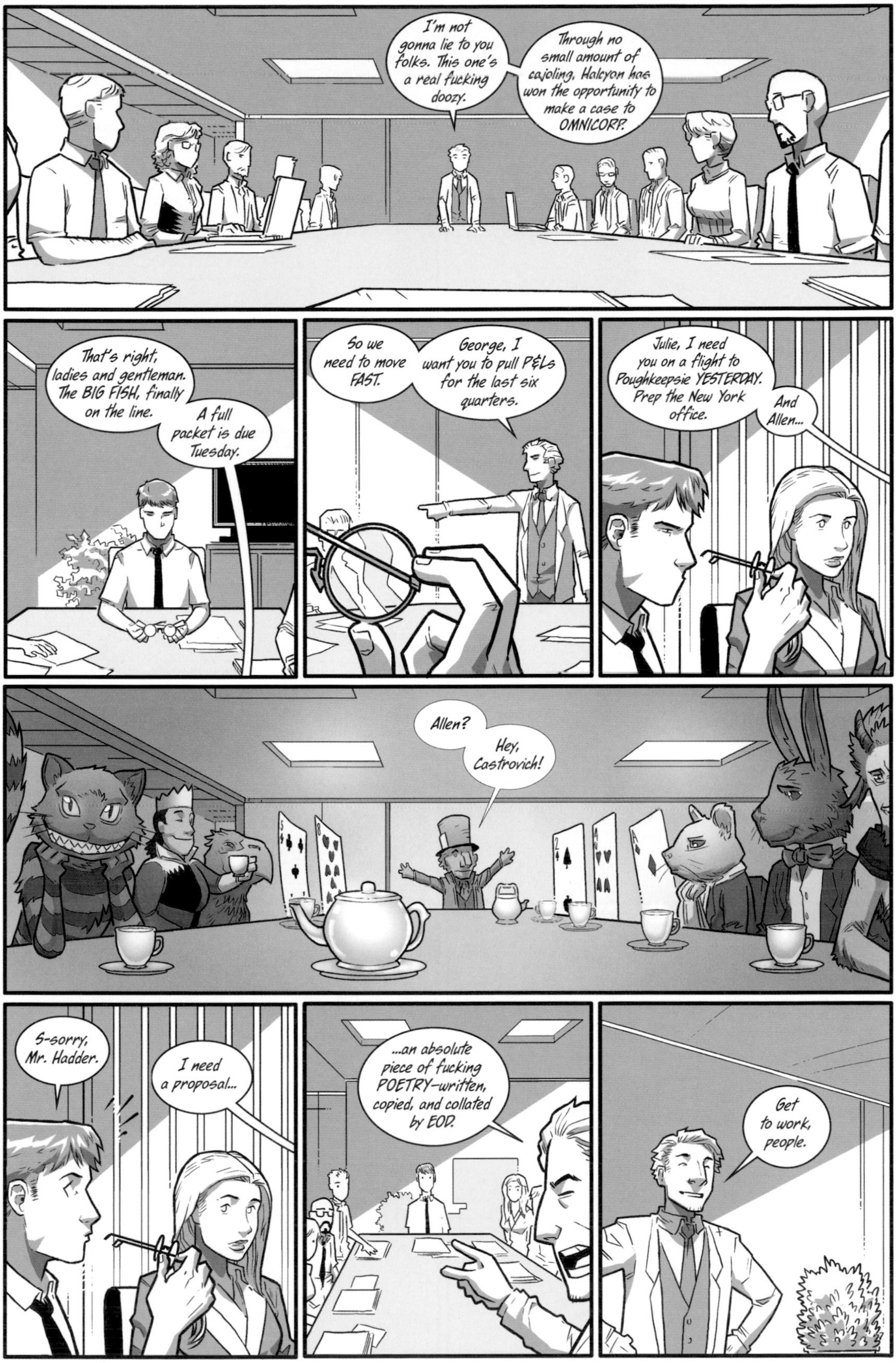
I'm not gonna lie to you folks. This one's a real fucking doozy.
Through no small amount of cajoling, Halcyon has won the opportunity to make a case to OMNICORP.
That's right, ladies and gentleman. The BIG FISH, finally on the line.
A full packet is due Tuesday.
So we need to move FAST.
George, I want you to pull P&Ls for the last six quarters.
Julie, I need you on a flight to Poughkeepsie YESTERDAY. Prep the New York office.
And Allen...
Allen?
Hey, Castrovich!
S-sorry, Mr. Hadder.
I need a proposal...
...an absolute piece of fucking POETRY—written, copied, and collated by EOD.
Get to work, people.

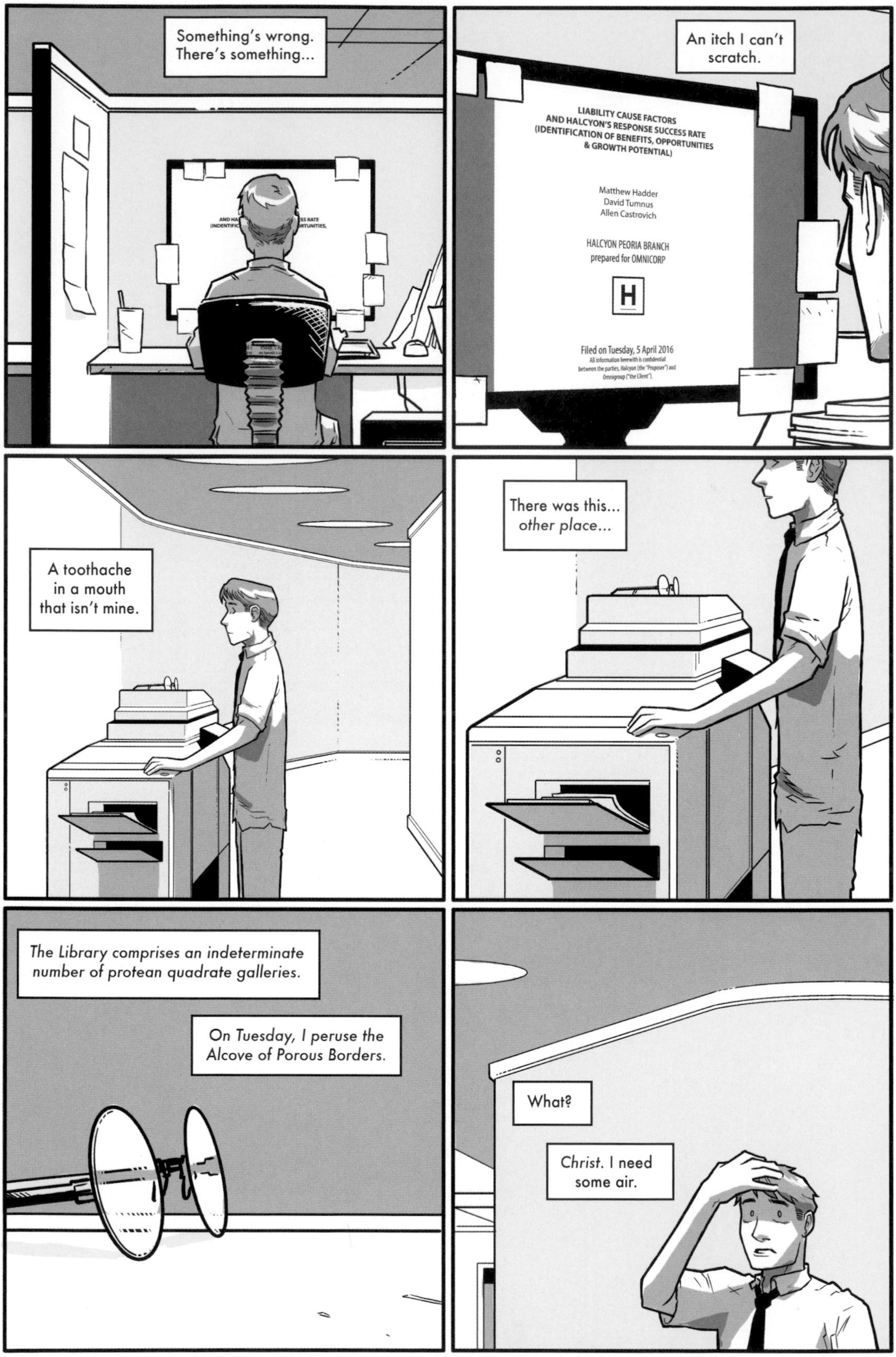
Something's wrong. There's something...
An itch I can't scratch.
LIABILITY CAUSE FACTORS
AND HALCYON'S RESPONSE SUCCESS RATE
(IDENTIFICATION OF BENEFITS, OPPORTUNITIES
& GROWTH POTENTIAL)
Matthew Hadder
David Tumnus
Allen Castrovich
HALCYON PEORIA BRANCH
prepared for OMNICORP
H
Filed on Tuesday, 5 April 2016
All information herewith is confidential between the parties, Halcyon (the "Proposer") and Omnigroup ("the Client").
A toothache in a mouth that isn't mine.
There was this... *other place...*
The Library comprises an indeterminate number of protean quadrate galleries.
On Tuesday, I peruse the Alcove of Porous Borders.
What?
Christ. I need some air.

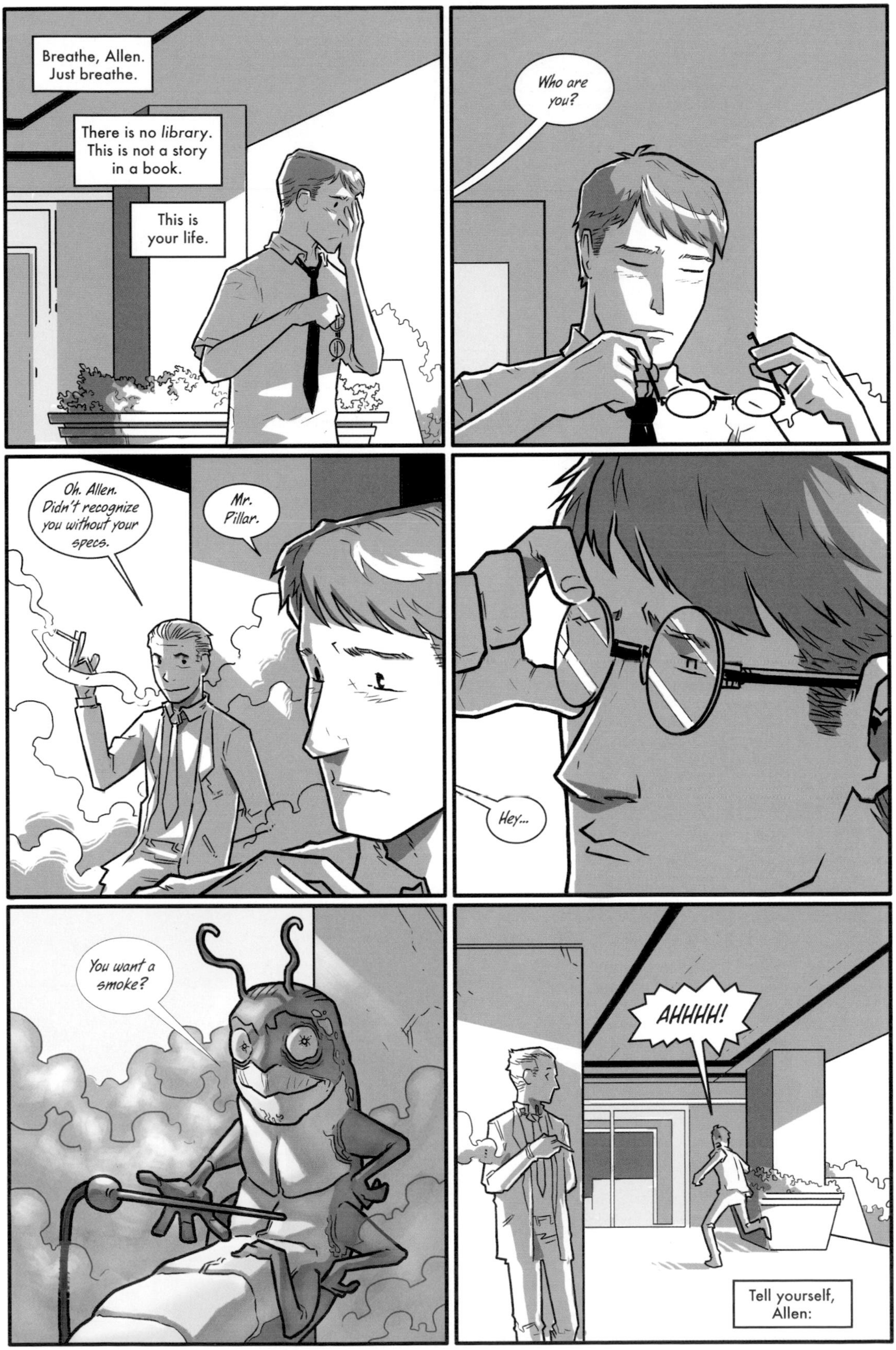
Breathe, Allen. Just breathe.
There is no *library*. This is not a story in a book.
This is your life.
Who are you?
Oh. Allen. Didn't recognize you without your specs.
Mr. Pillar.
Hey...
You want a smoke?
AHHHH!
Tell yourself, Allen:

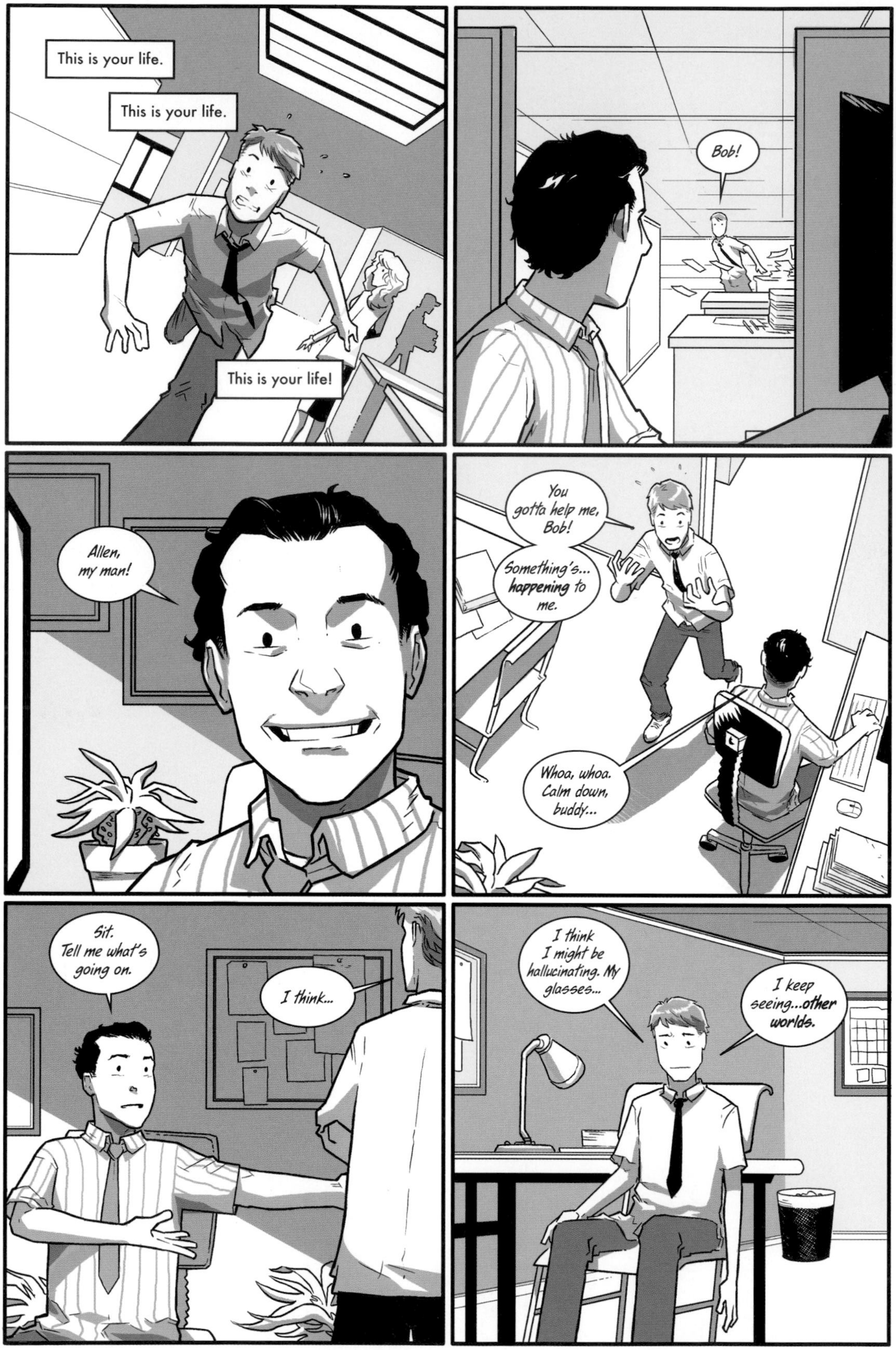
This is your life.
This is your life.
This is your life!
Bob!
Allen, my man!
You gotta help me, Bob!
Something's... **happening** to me.
Whoa, whoa. Calm down, buddy...
Sit. Tell me what's going on.
I think...
I think I might be hallucinating. My glasses...
I keep seeing... **other worlds.**

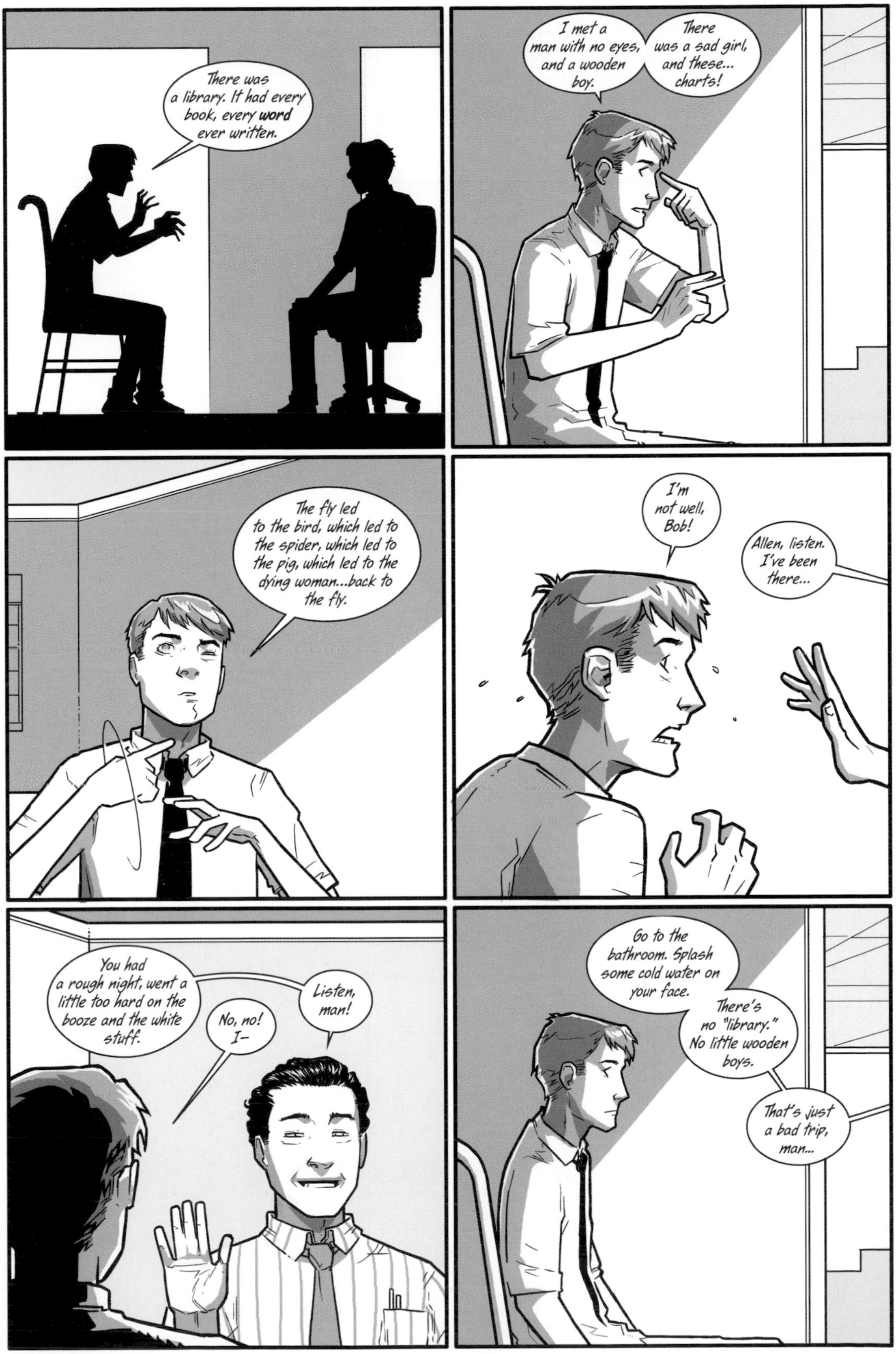
There was a library. It had every book, every **word** ever written.
I met a man with no eyes, and a wooden boy.
There was a sad girl, and these... charts!
The fly led to the bird, which led to the spider, which led to the pig, which led to the dying woman...back to the fly.
I'm not well, Bob!
Allen, listen. I've been there...
You had a rough night, went a little too hard on the booze and the white stuff.
No, no! I–
Listen, man!
Go to the bathroom. Splash some cold water on your face.
There's no "library." No little wooden boys.
That's just a bad trip, man...

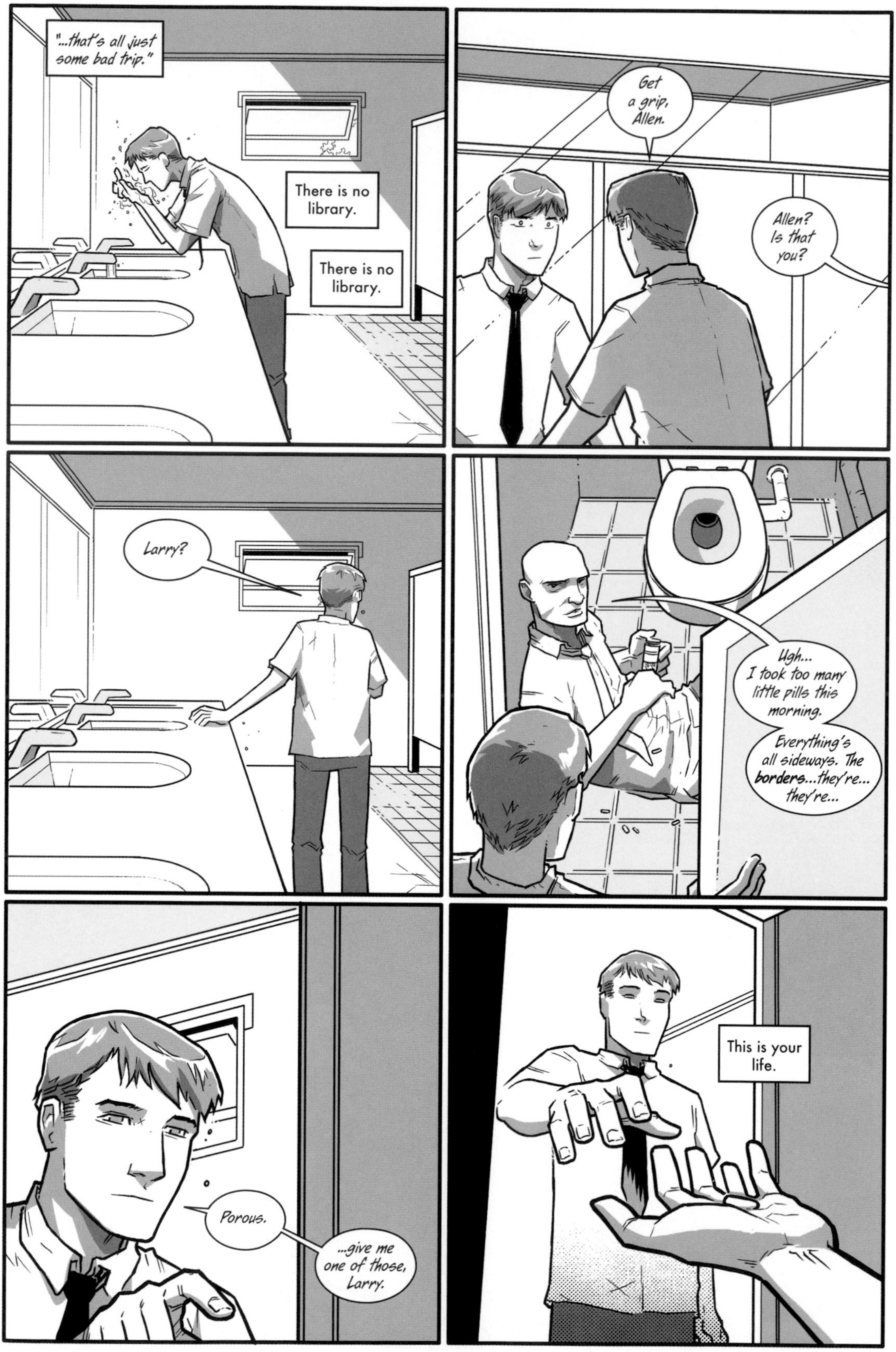
"...that's all just some bad trip."
There is no library.
There is no library.
Get a grip, Allen.
Allen? Is that you?
Larry?
Ugh... I took too many little pills this morning.
Everything's all sideways. The **borders**...they're... they're...
Porous.
...give me one of those, Larry.
This is your life.

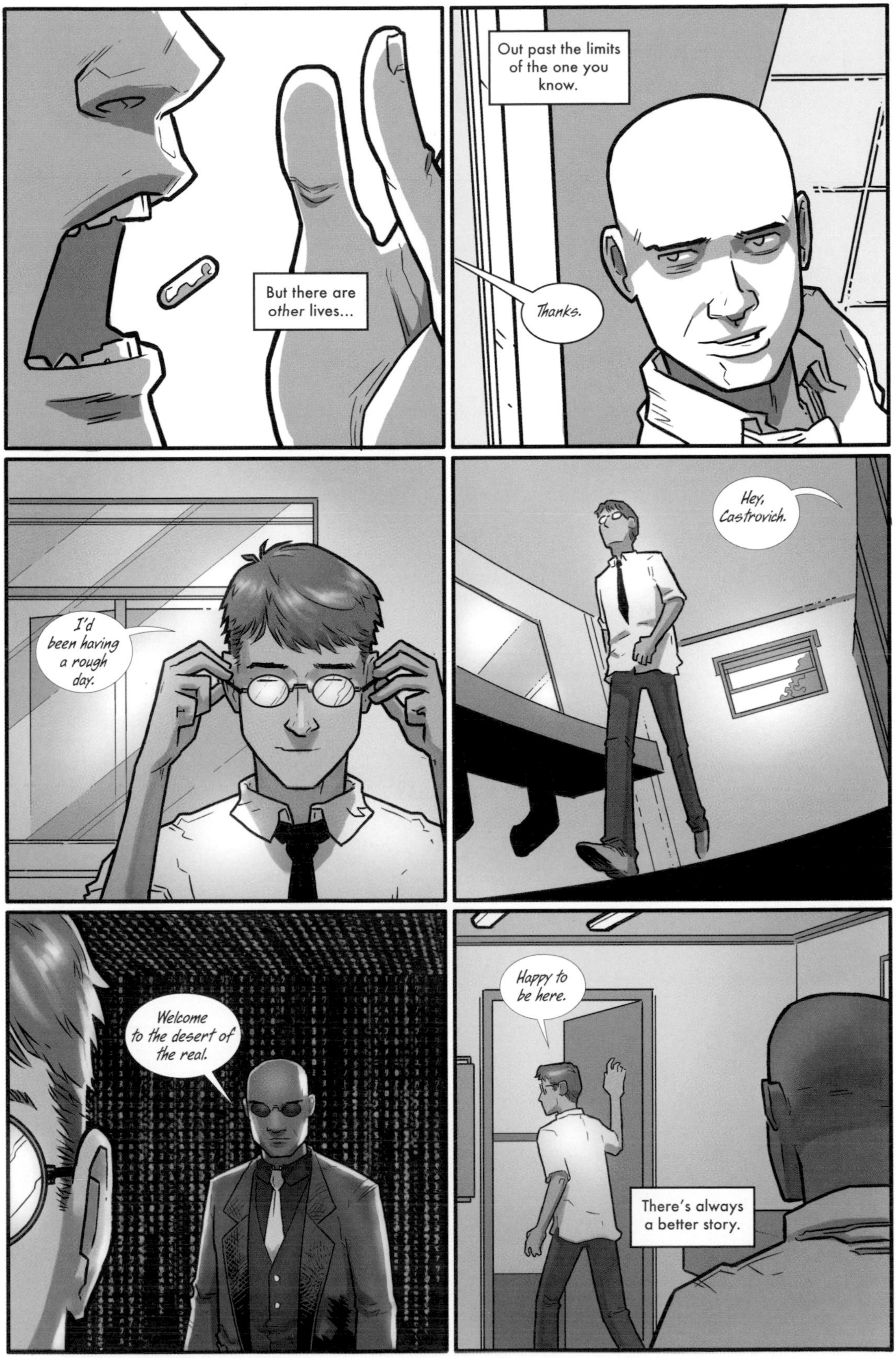
But there are other lives...
Out past the limits of the one you know.
Thanks.
I'd been having a rough day.
Hey, Castrovich.
Welcome to the desert of the real.
Happy to be here.
There's always a better story.

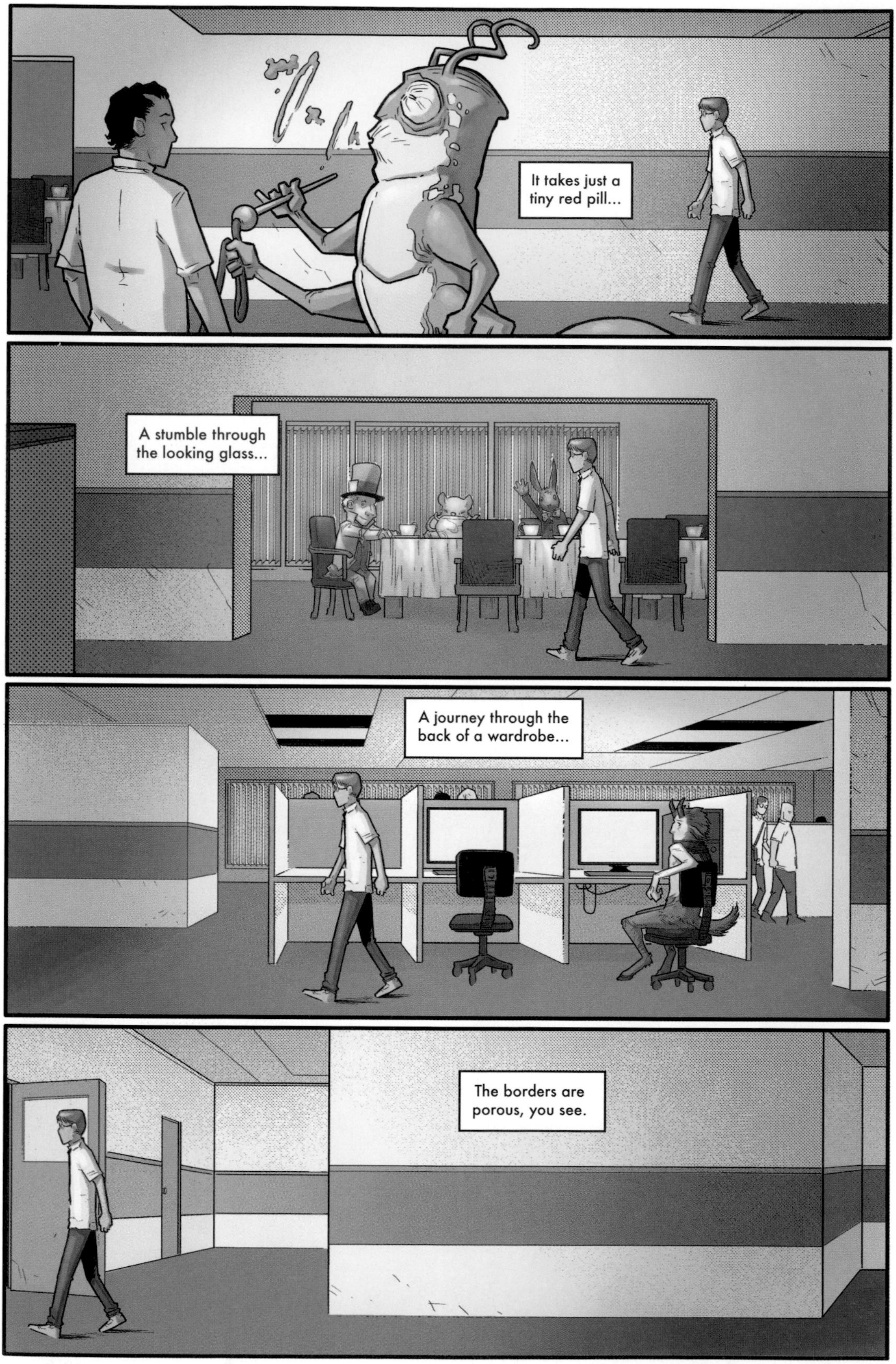

It takes just a tiny red pill...
A stumble through the looking glass...
A journey through the back of a wardrobe...
The borders are porous, you see.

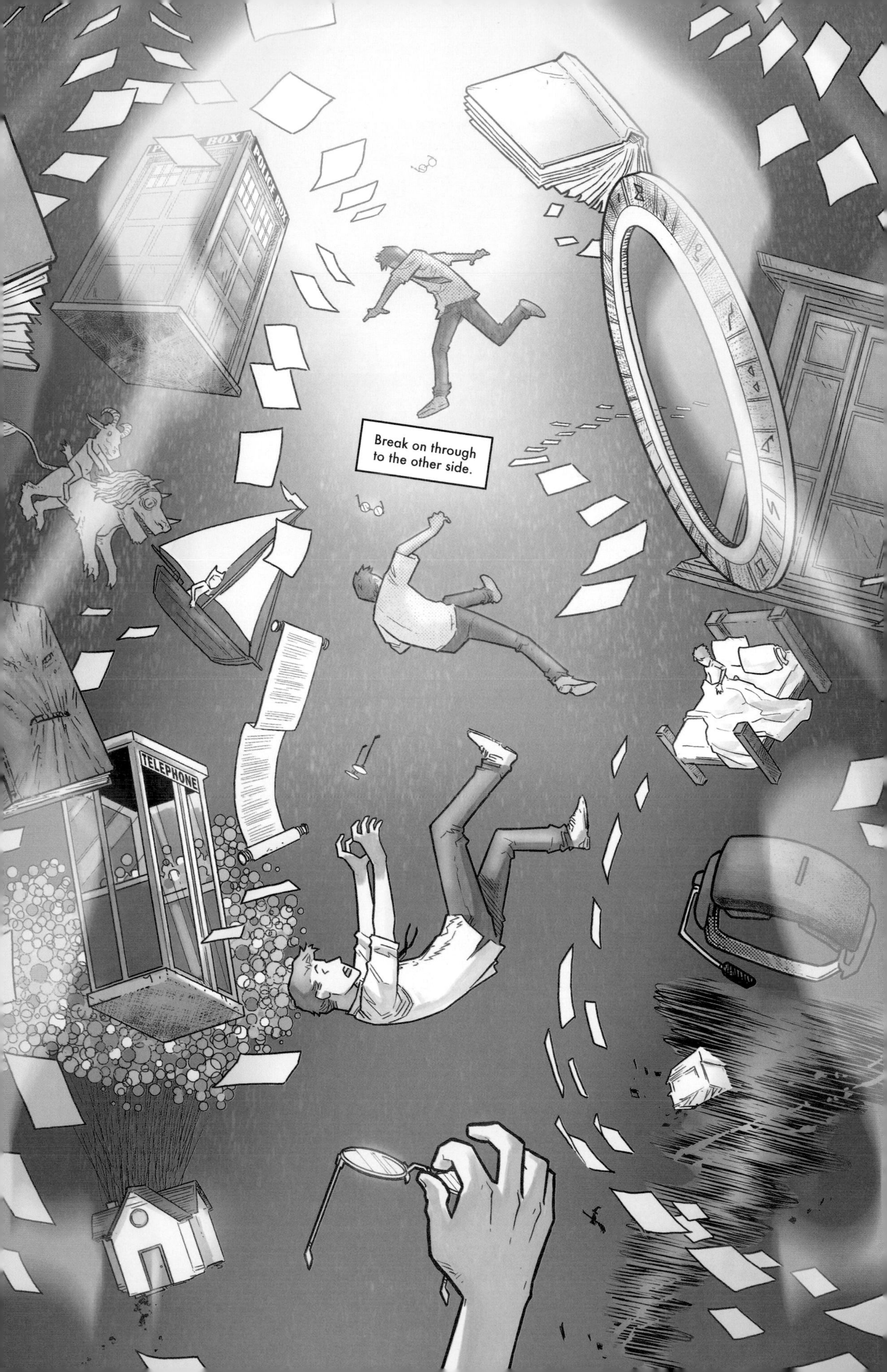
Break on through
to the other side.
POLICE BOX
TELEPHONE

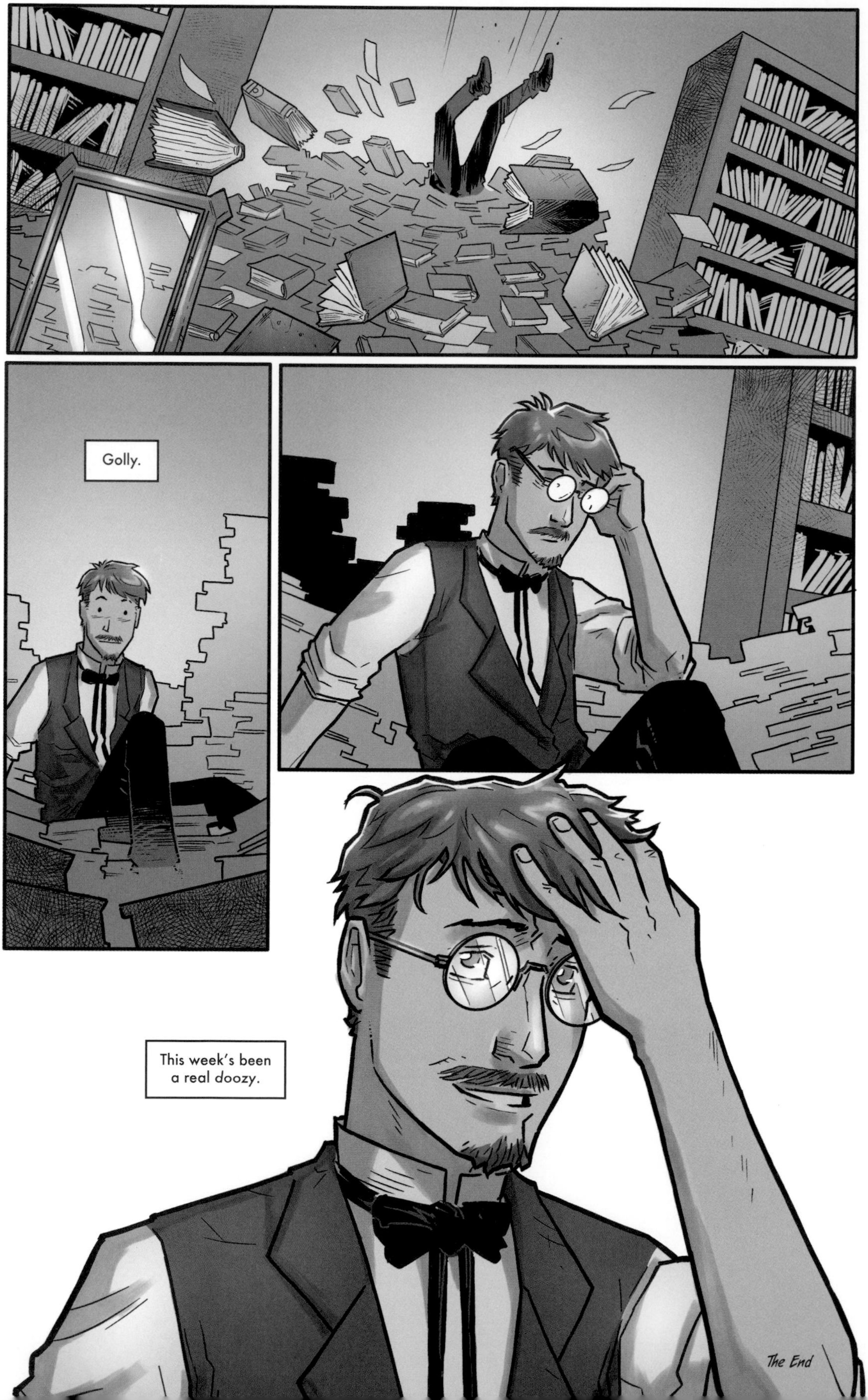
Golly.
This week's been a real *doozy*.
The End

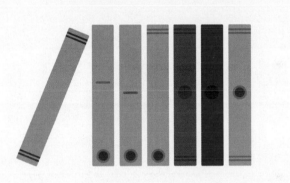

WEDNESDAY

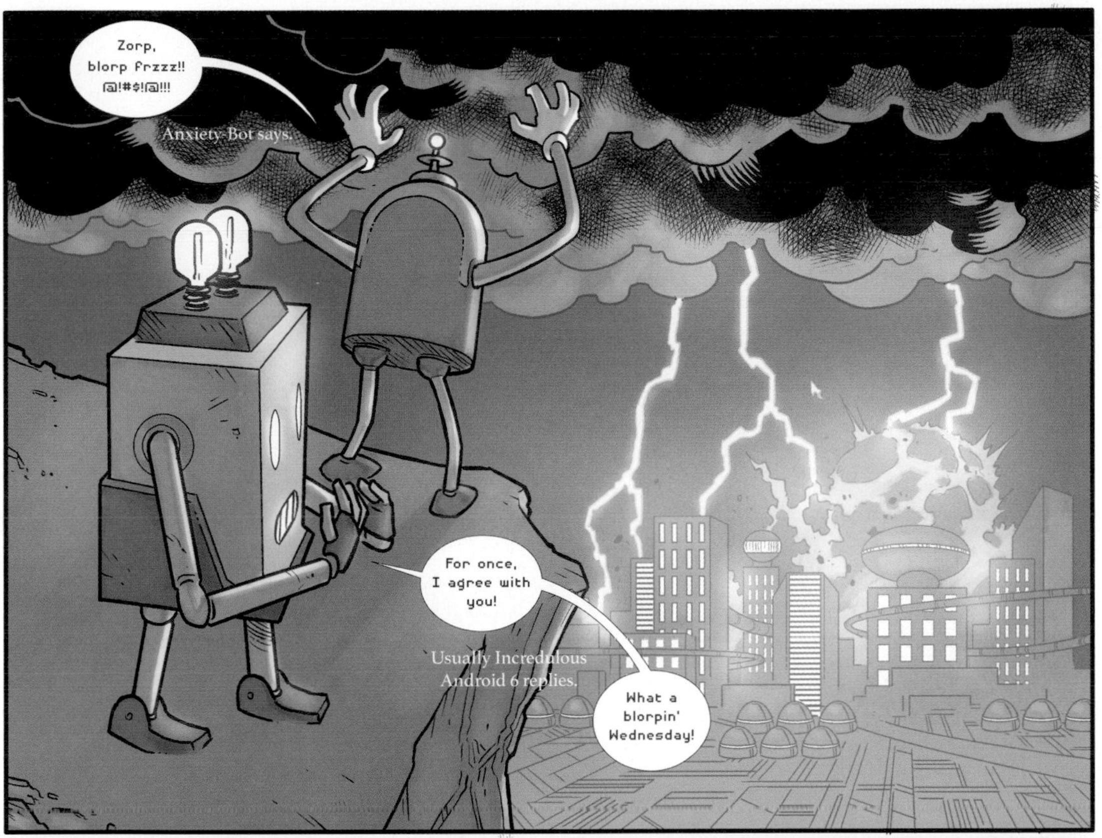
Zorp, blorp frzzz!! @!#$!@!!!
Anxiety-Bot says.
For once, I agree with you!
Usually Incredulous Android 6 replies.
What a blorpin' Wednesday!

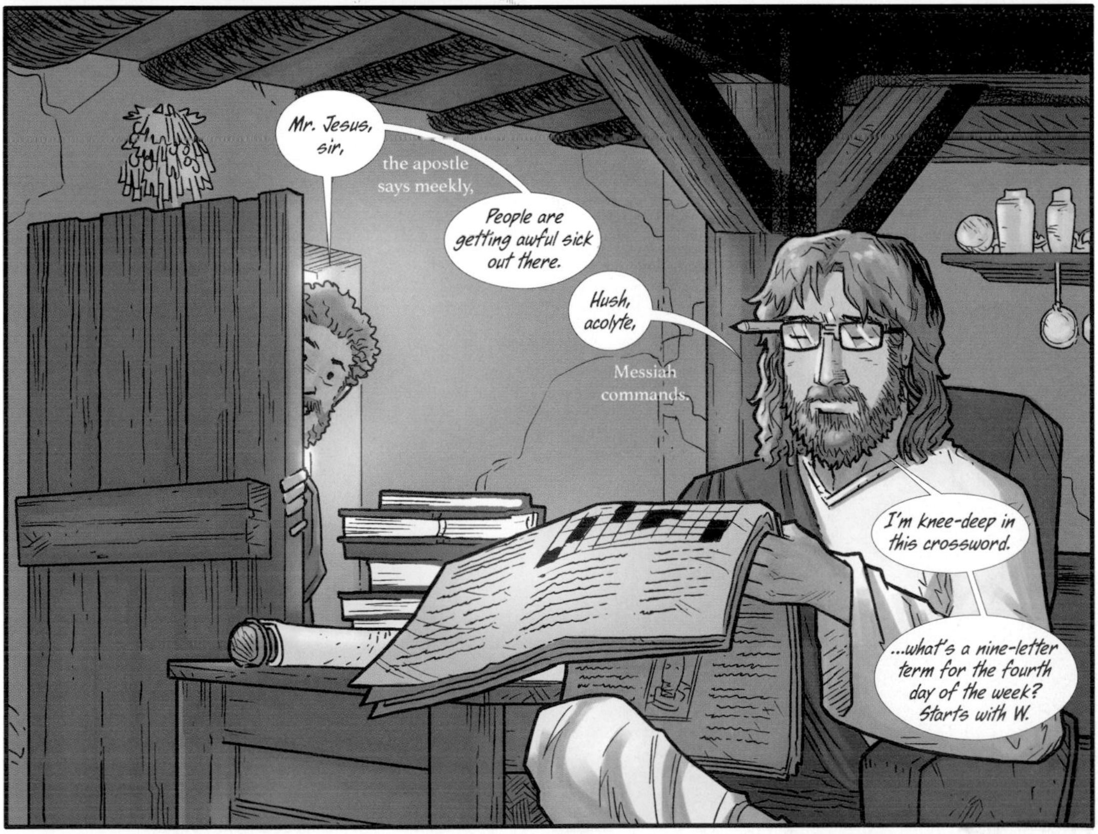
Mr. Jesus, sir,
the apostle says meekly,
People are getting awful sick out there.
Hush, acolyte,
Messiah commands.
I'm knee-deep in this crossword.
...what's a nine-letter term for the fourth day of the week? Starts with W.

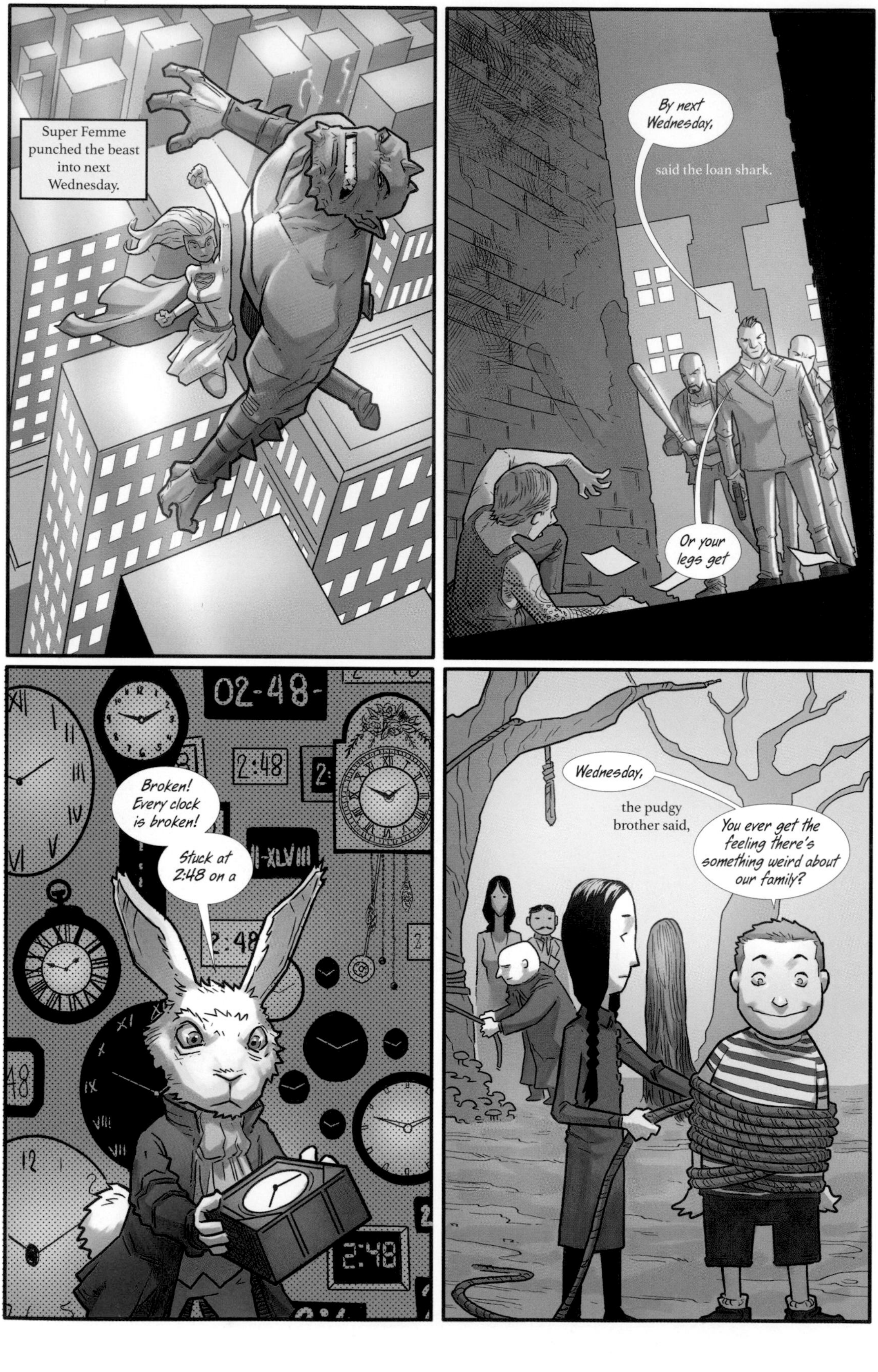
Super Femme punched the beast into next Wednesday.
By next Wednesday,
said the loan shark.
Or your legs get
Broken! Every clock is broken!
Stuck at 2:48 on a
Wednesday,
the pudgy brother said,
You ever get the feeling there's something weird about our family?

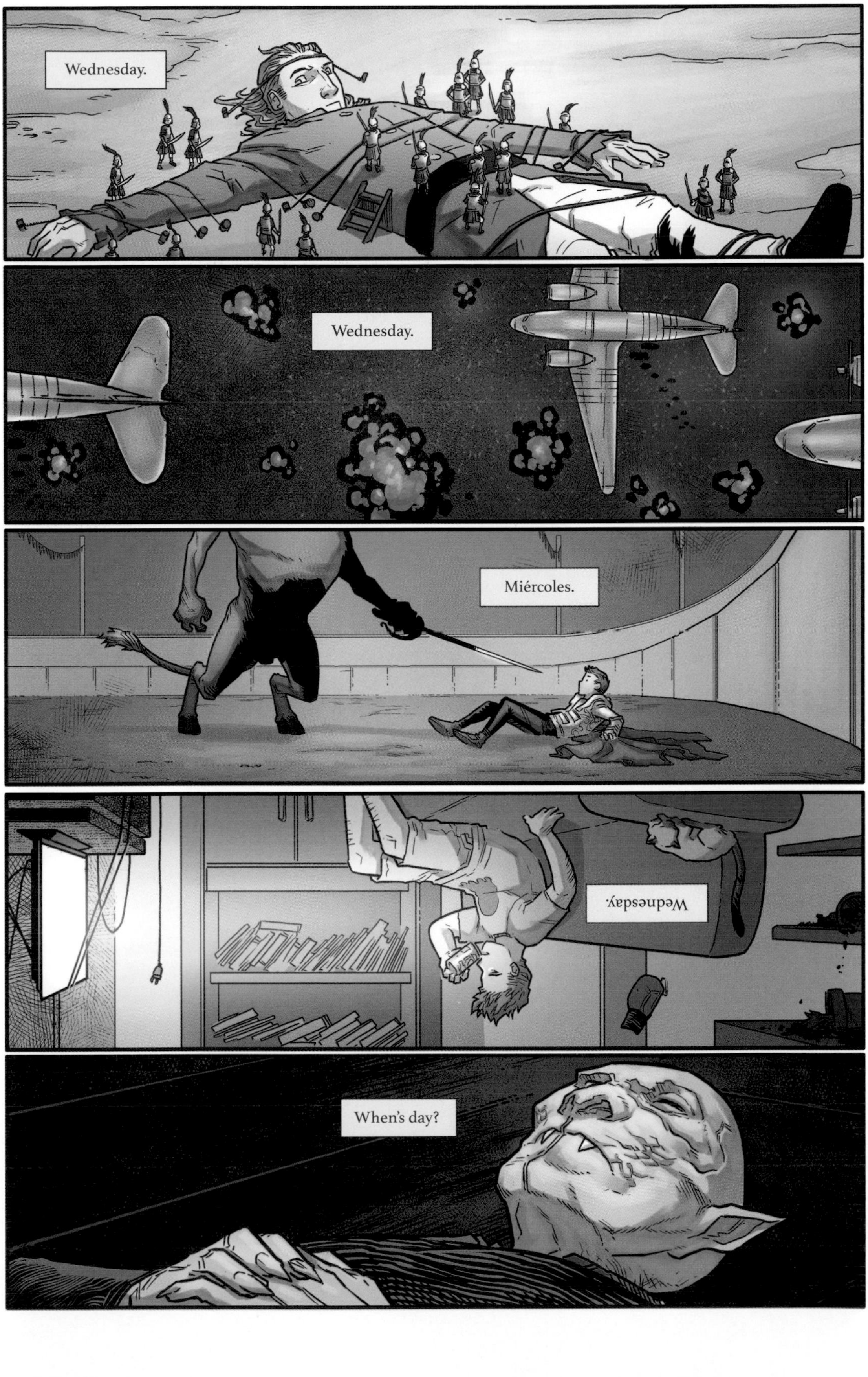
Wednesday.
Wednesday.
Miércoles.
Wednesday.
When's day?

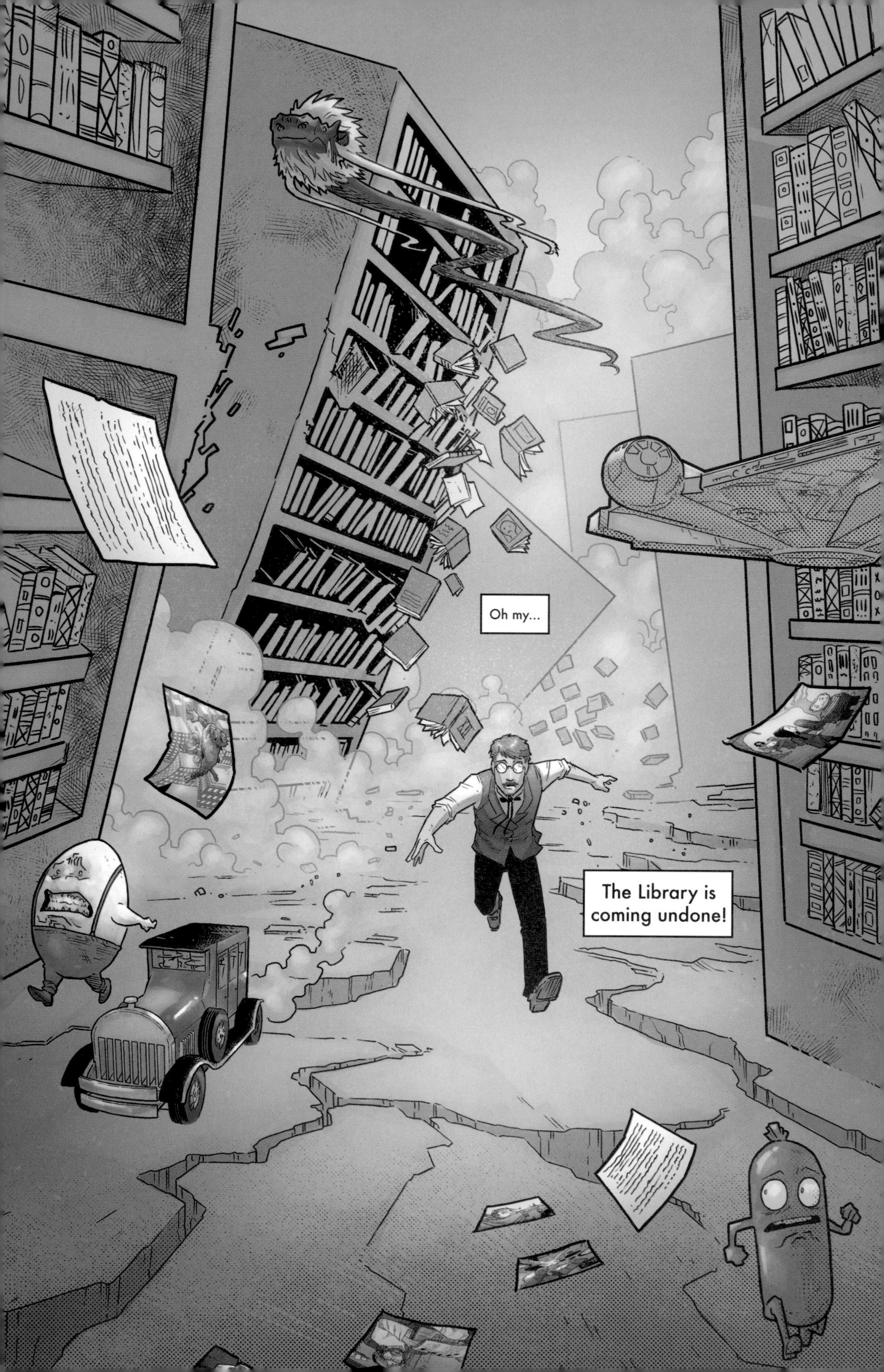
Oh my...
The Library is coming undone!

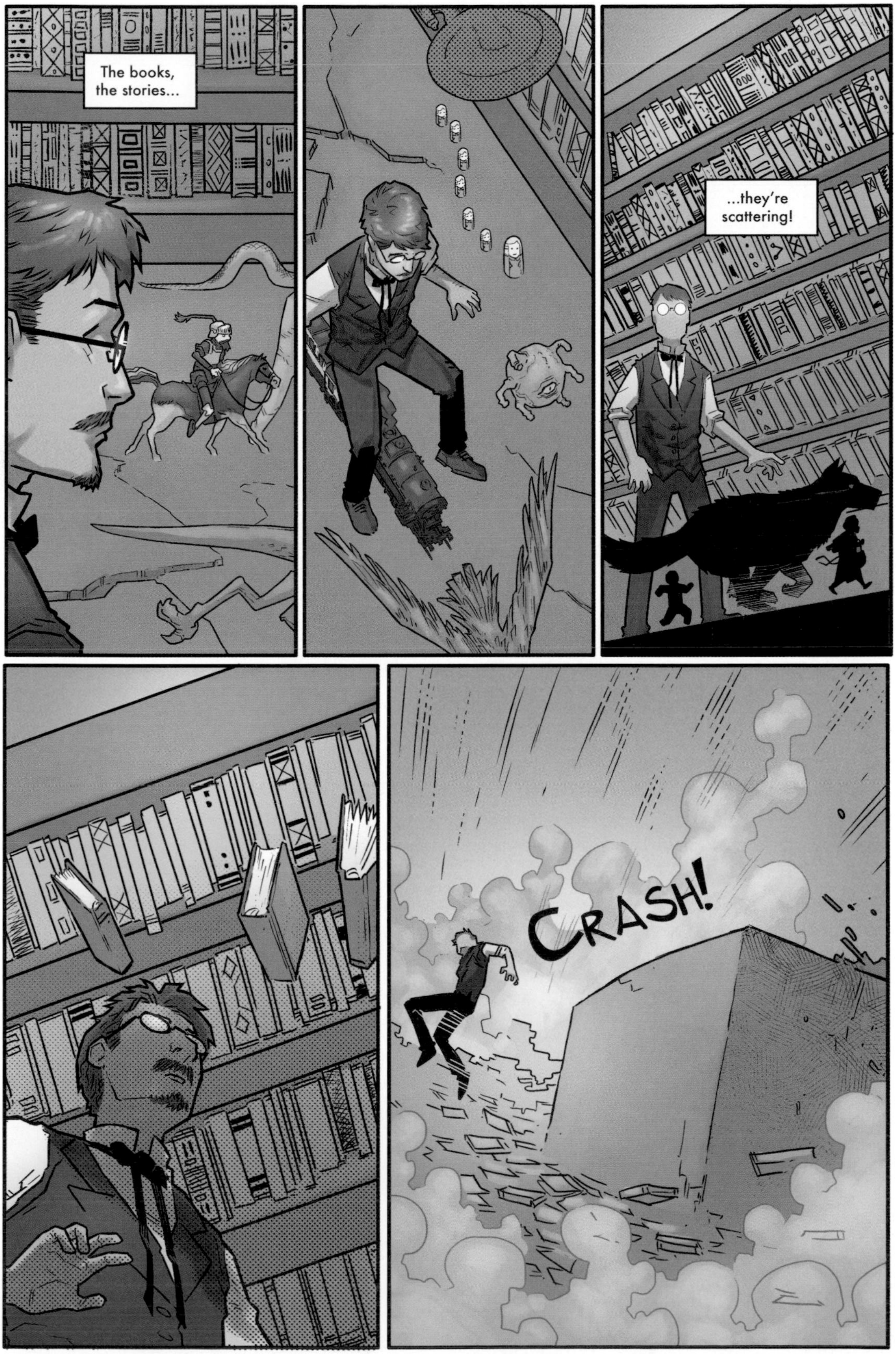
The books, the stories...
...they're scattering!
CRASH!

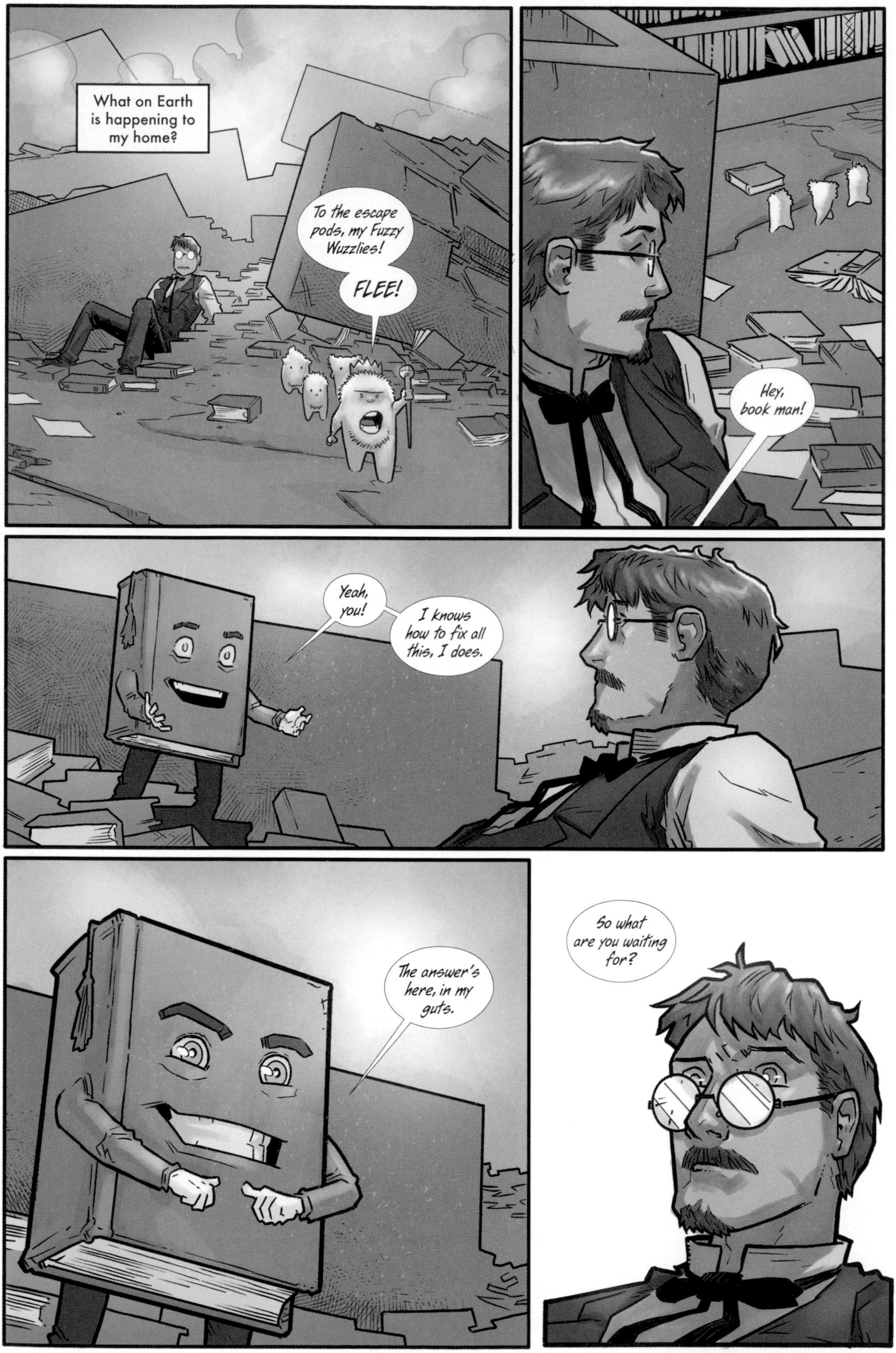
What on Earth is happening to my home?
To the escape pods, my Fuzzy Wuzzlies!
FLEE!
Hey, book man!
Yeah, you!
I knows how to fix all this, I does.
The answer's here, in my guts.
So what are you waiting for?

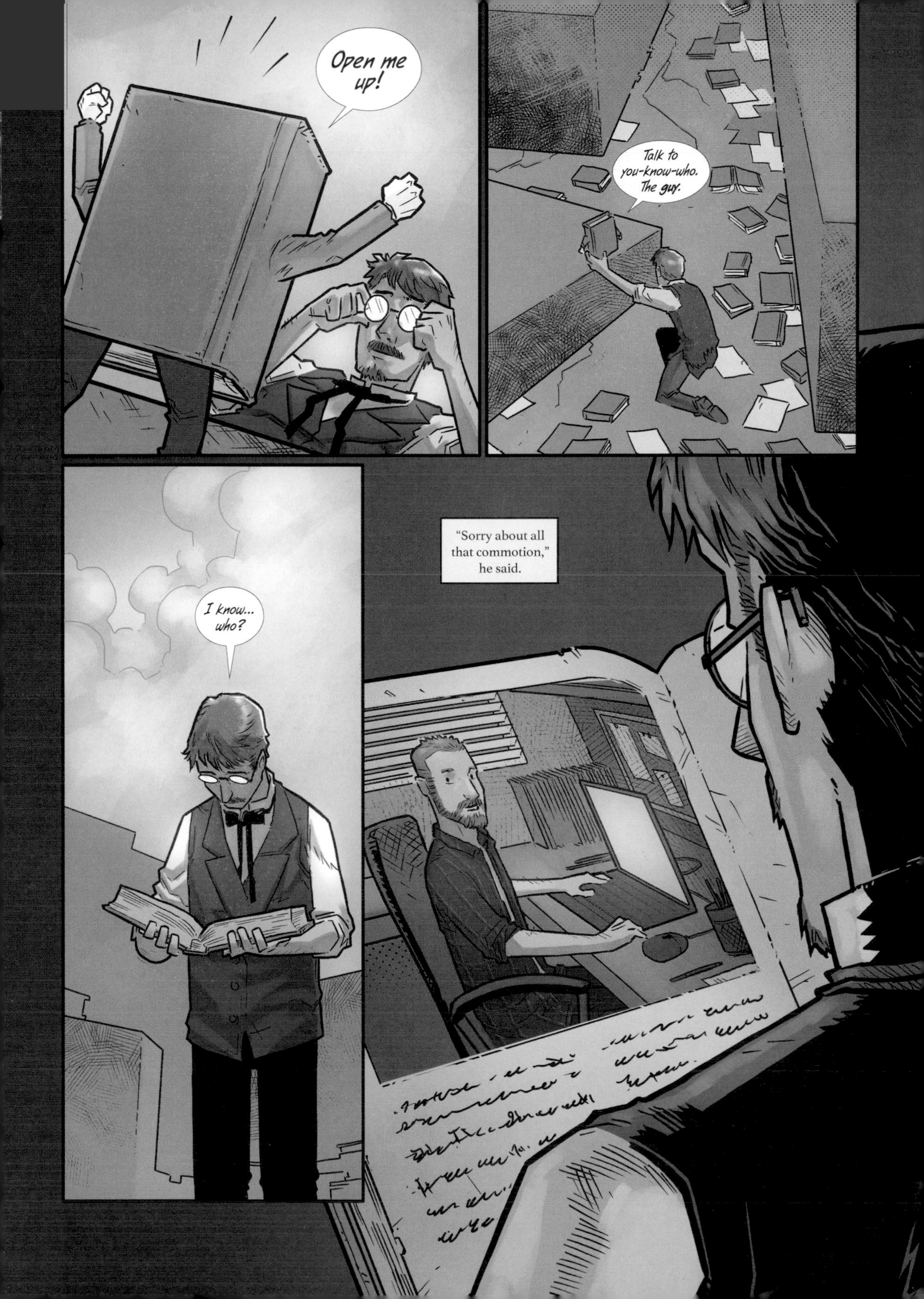
Open me up!
Talk to you-know-who. The guy.
I know... who?
"Sorry about all that commotion," he said.

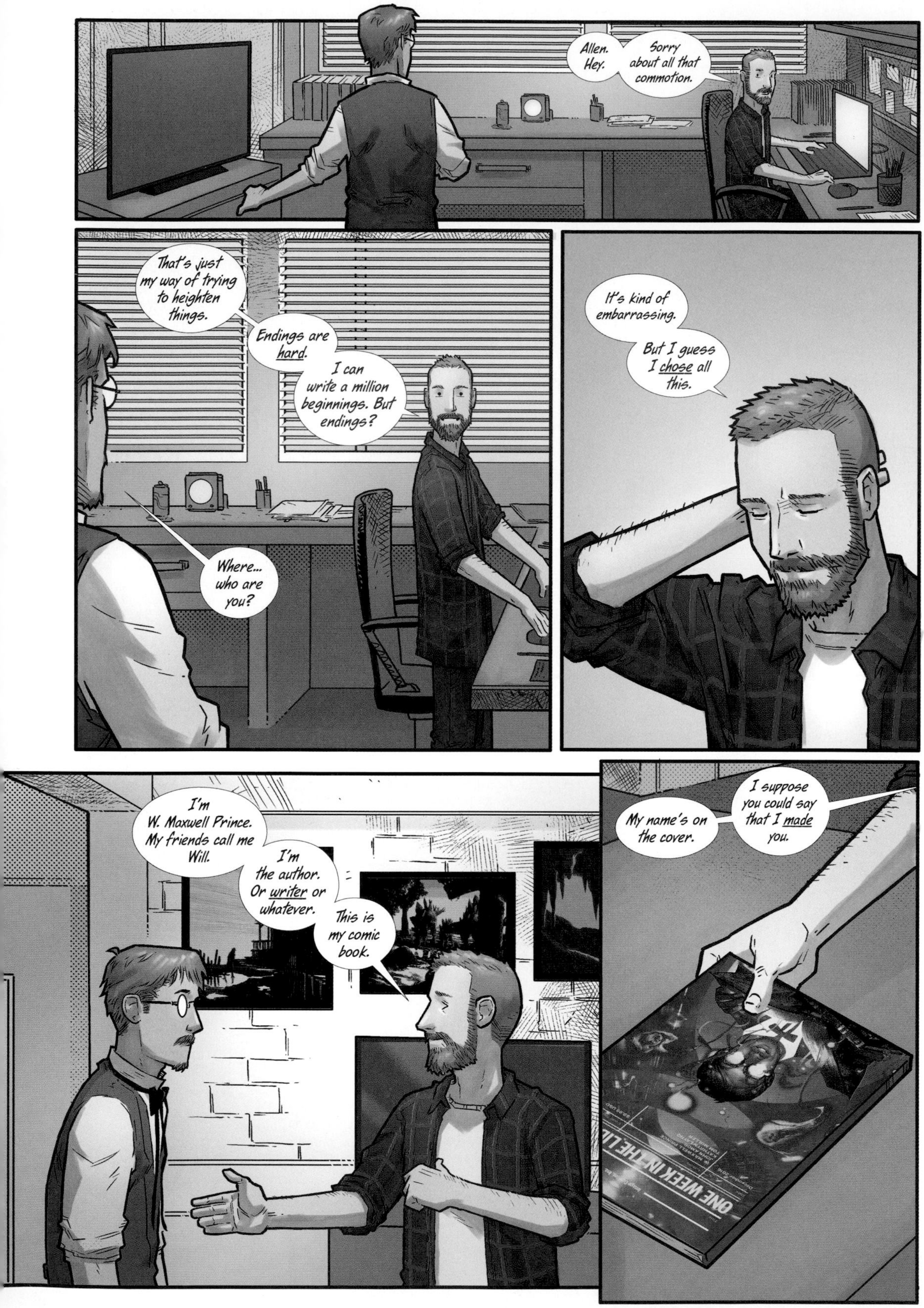
Allen. Hey.
Sorry about all that commotion.
That's just my way of trying to heighten things.
Endings are hard.
I can write a million beginnings. But endings?
Where... who are you?
It's kind of embarrassing.
But I guess I chose all this.
I'm W. Maxwell Prince. My friends call me Will.
I'm the author. Or writer or whatever.
This is my comic book.
My name's on the cover.
I suppose you could say that I made you.
ONE WEEK IN THE LI

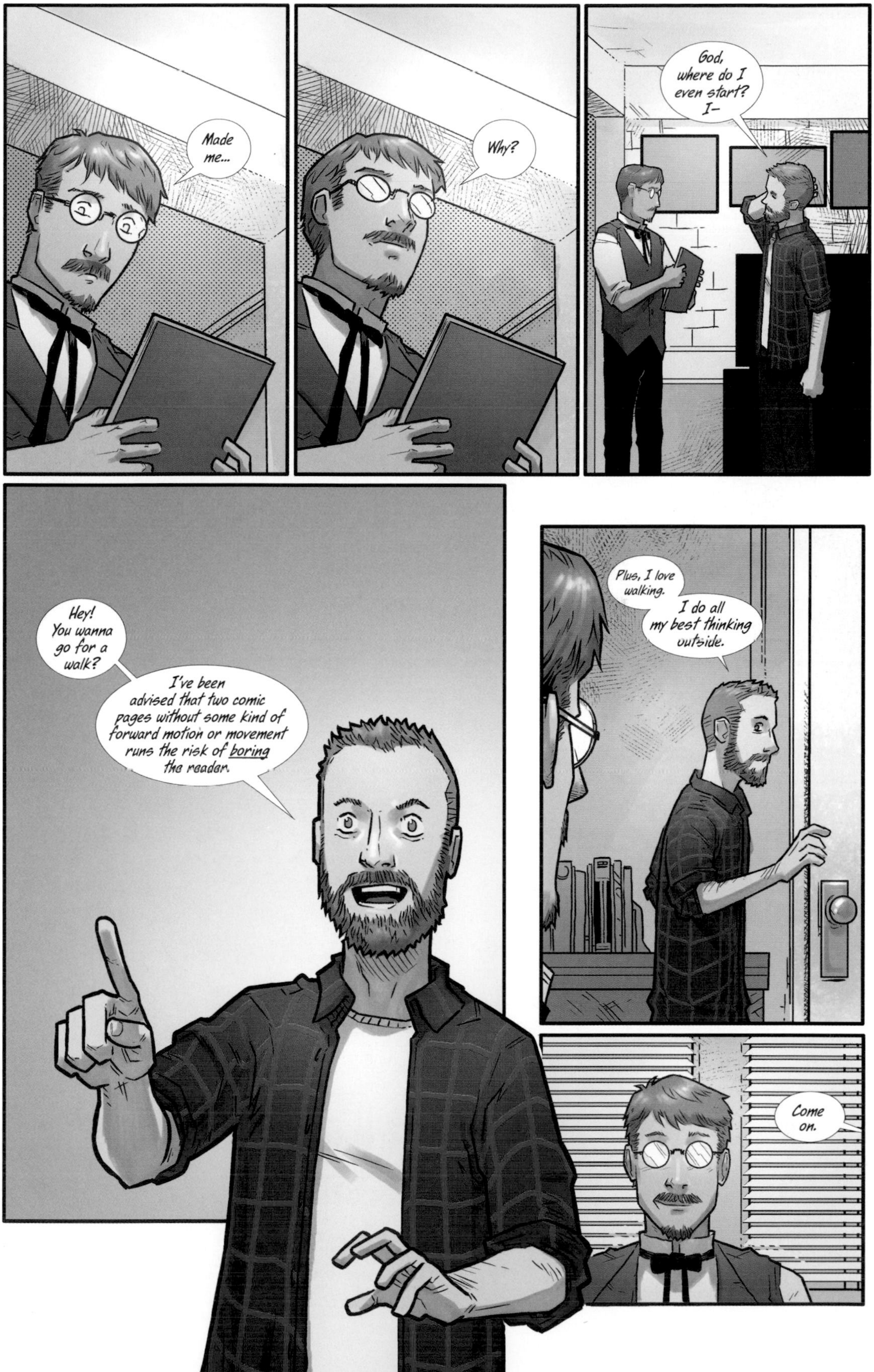
Made me...
Why?
God, where do I even start? I–
Hey! You wanna go for a walk?
I've been advised that two comic pages without some kind of forward motion or movement runs the risk of boring the reader.
Plus, I love walking.
I do all my best thinking outside.
Come on.

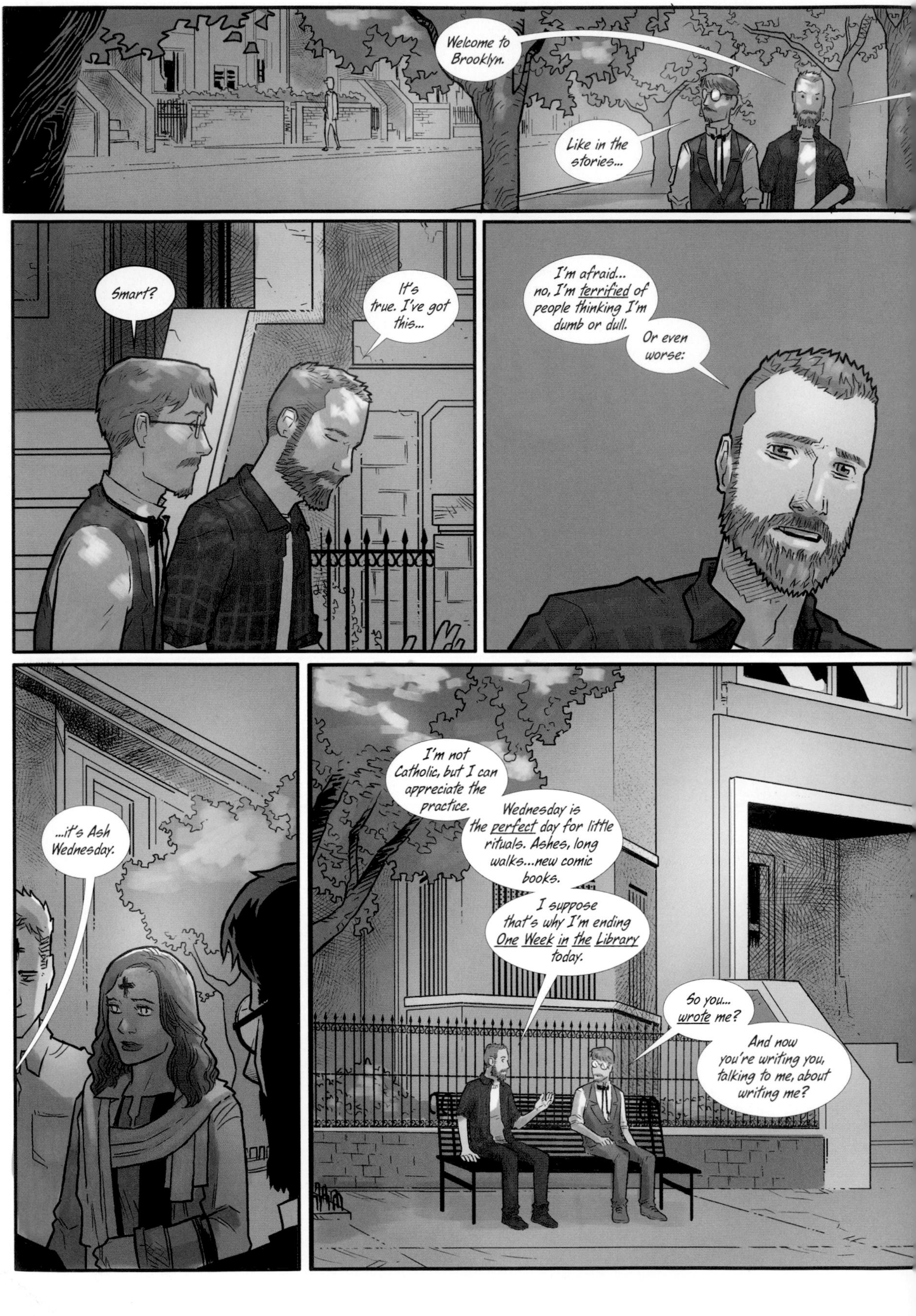
Welcome to Brooklyn.
Like in the stories...
Smart?
It's true. I've got this...
I'm afraid... no, I'm terrified of people thinking I'm dumb or dull.
Or even worse:
...it's Ash Wednesday.
I'm not Catholic, but I can appreciate the practice.
Wednesday is the perfect day for little rituals. Ashes, long walks...new comic books.
I suppose that's why I'm ending One Week in the Library today.
So you... wrote me?
And now you're writing you, talking to me, about writing me?

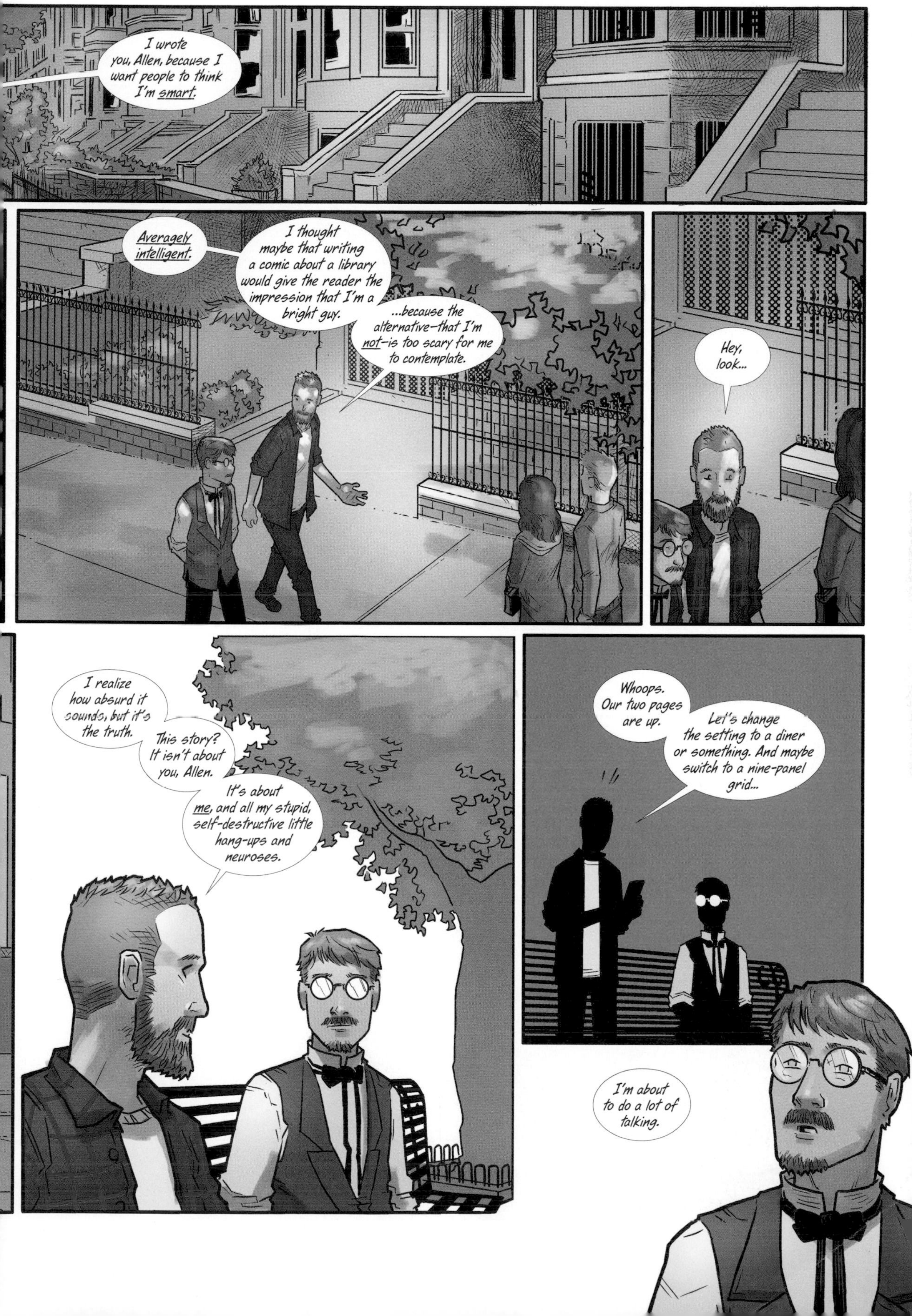
I wrote you, Allen, because I want people to think I'm smart.
Averagely intelligent.
I thought maybe that writing a comic about a library would give the reader the impression that I'm a bright guy.
...because the alternative—that I'm not—is too scary for me to contemplate.
Hey, look...
I realize how absurd it sounds, but it's the truth.
This story? It isn't about you, Allen.
It's about me, and all my stupid, self-destructive little hang-ups and neuroses.
Whoops. Our two pages are up.
Let's change the setting to a diner or something. And maybe switch to a nine-panel grid...
I'm about to do a lot of talking.

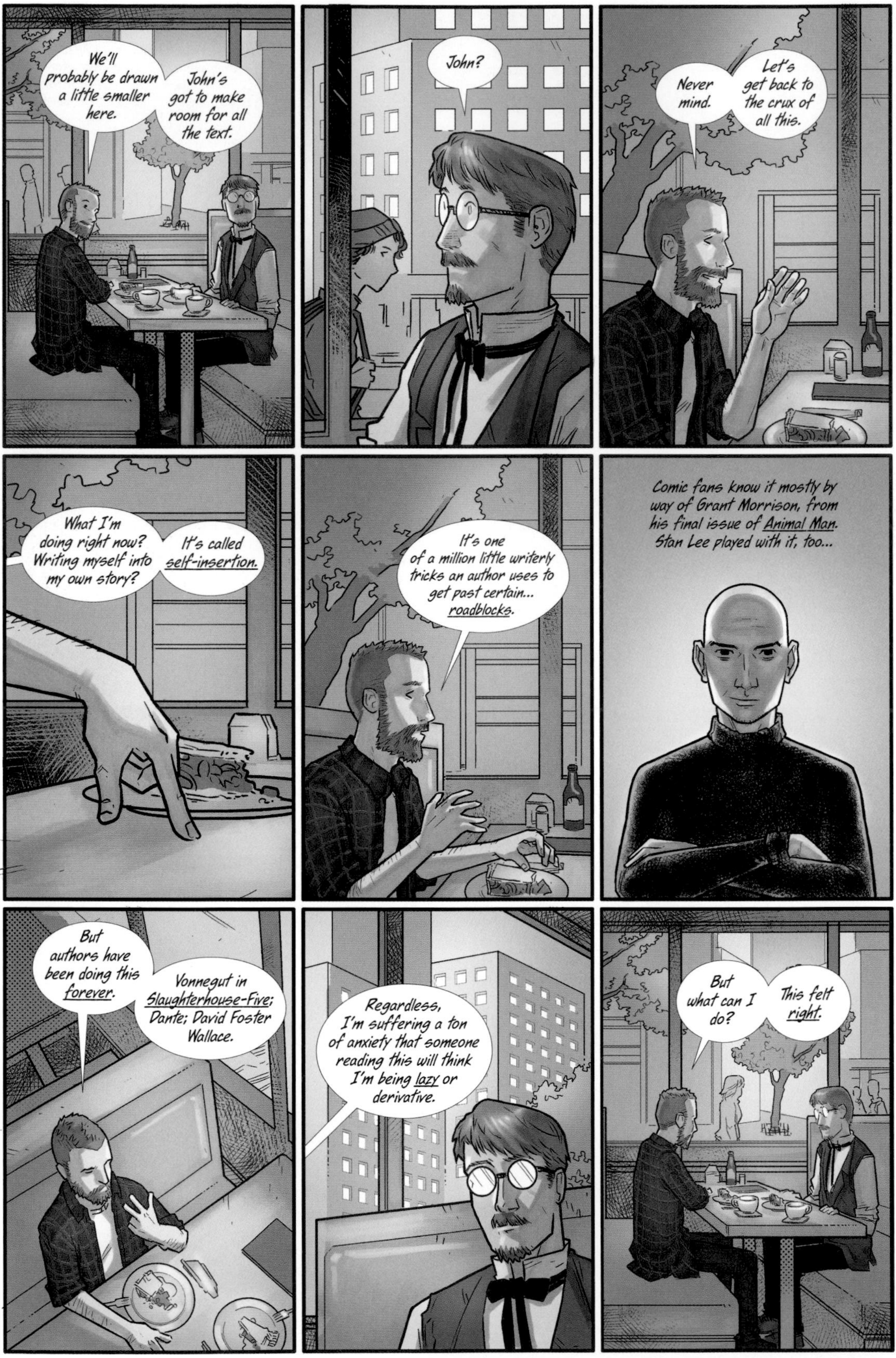
We'll probably be drawn a little smaller here.
John's got to make room for all the text.
John?
Never mind.
Let's get back to the crux of all this.
What I'm doing right now? Writing myself into my own story?
It's called self-insertion.
It's one of a million little writerly tricks an author uses to get past certain... roadblocks.
Comic fans know it mostly by way of Grant Morrison, from his final issue of Animal Man. Stan Lee played with it, too...
But authors have been doing this forever.
Vonnegut in Slaughterhouse-Five; Dante; David Foster Wallace.
Regardless, I'm suffering a ton of anxiety that someone reading this will think I'm being lazy or derivative.
But what can I do?
This felt right.

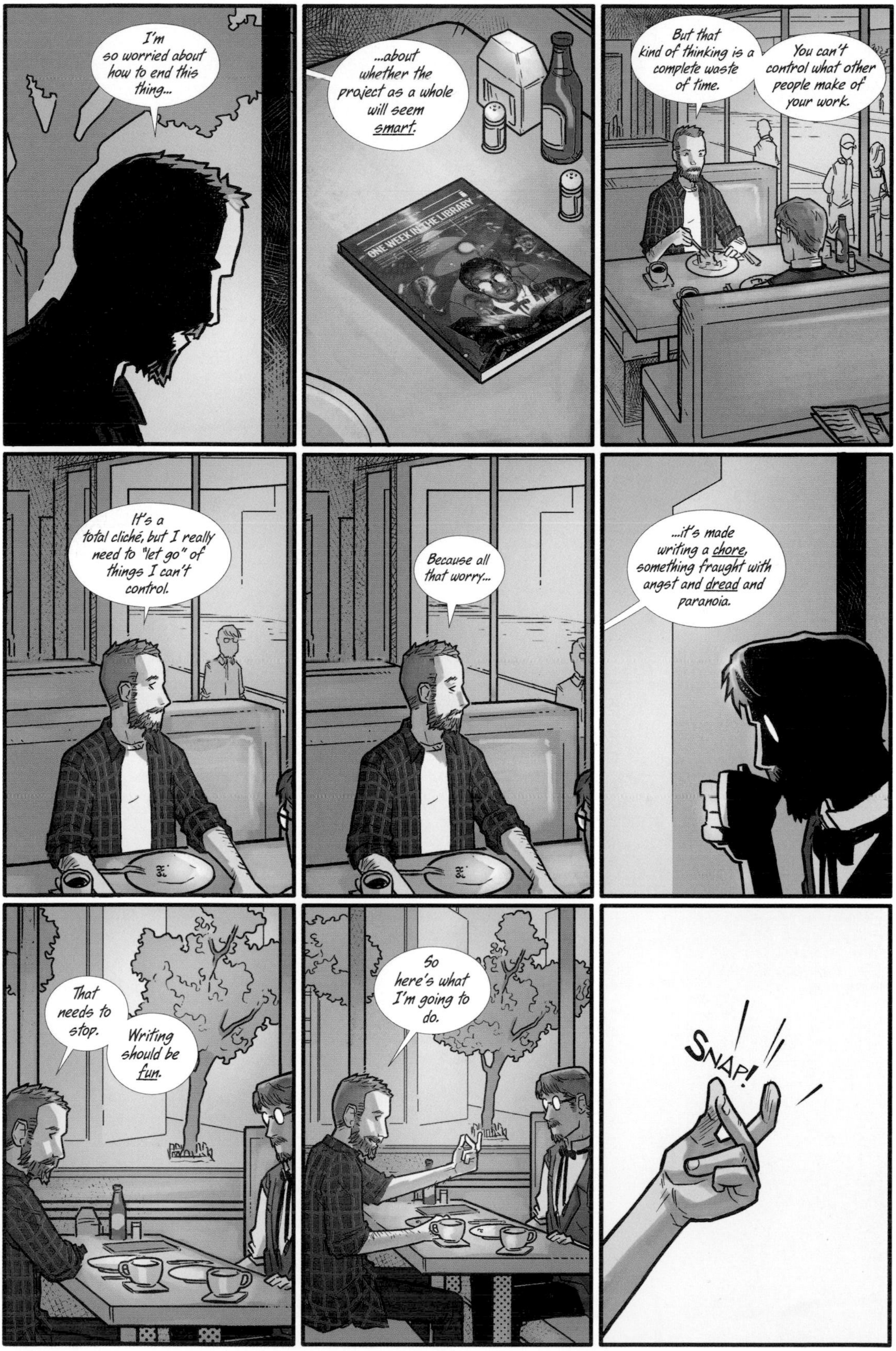
I'm so worried about how to end this thing...
...about whether the project as a whole will seem smart.
ONE WEEK IN THE LIBRARY
But that kind of thinking is a complete waste of time.
You can't control what other people make of your work.
It's a total cliché, but I really need to "let go" of things I can't control.
Because all that worry...
...it's made writing a chore, something fraught with angst and dread and paranoia.
That needs to stop.
Writing should be fun.
So here's what I'm going to do.
SNAP!

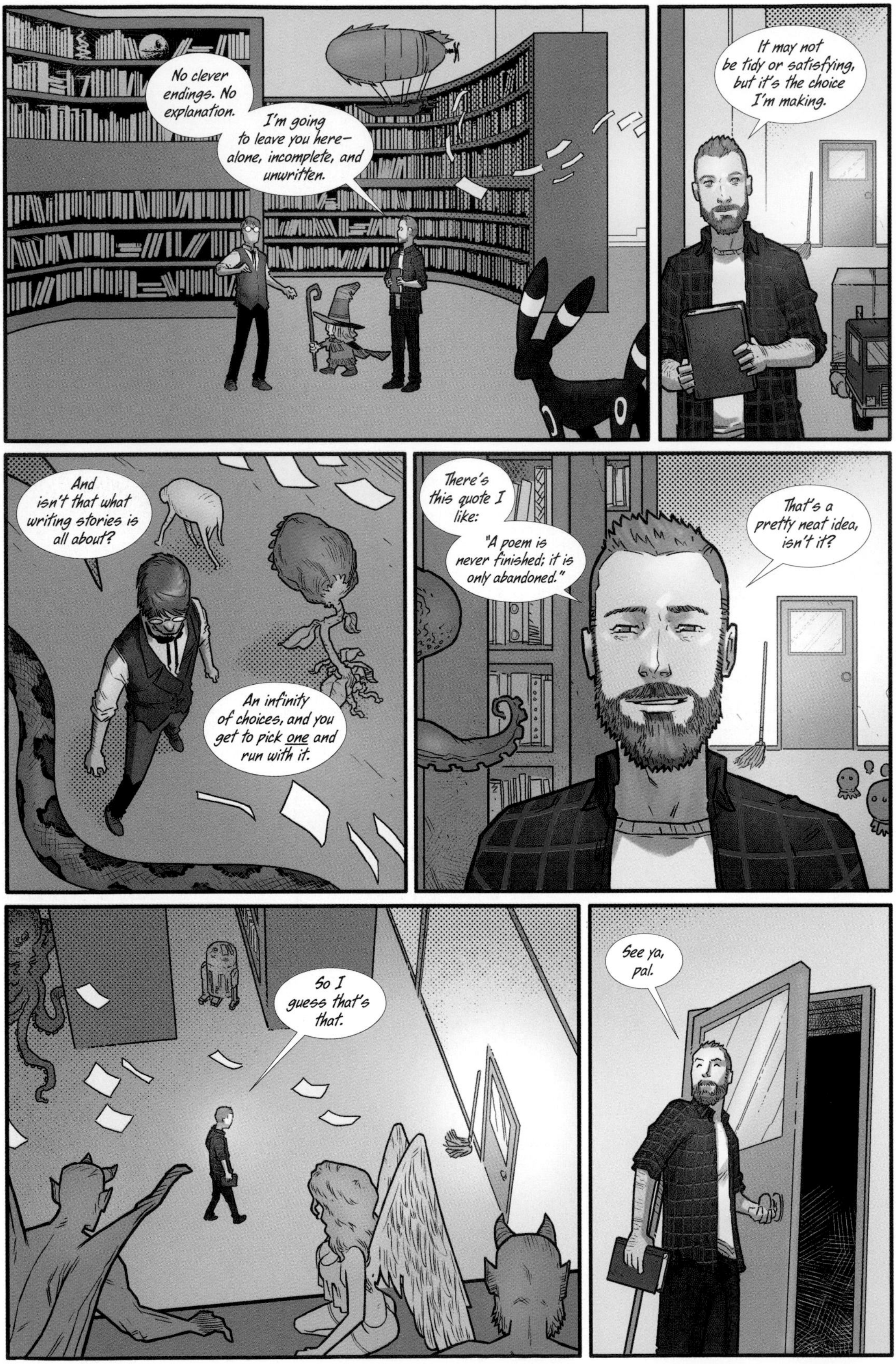
No clever endings. No explanation.
I'm going to leave you here—alone, incomplete, and unwritten.
It may not be tidy or satisfying, but it's the choice I'm making.
And isn't that what writing stories is all about?
An infinity of choices, and you get to pick one and run with it.
There's this quote I like:
"A poem is never finished; it is only abandoned."
That's a pretty neat idea, isn't it?
So I guess that's that.
See ya, pal.

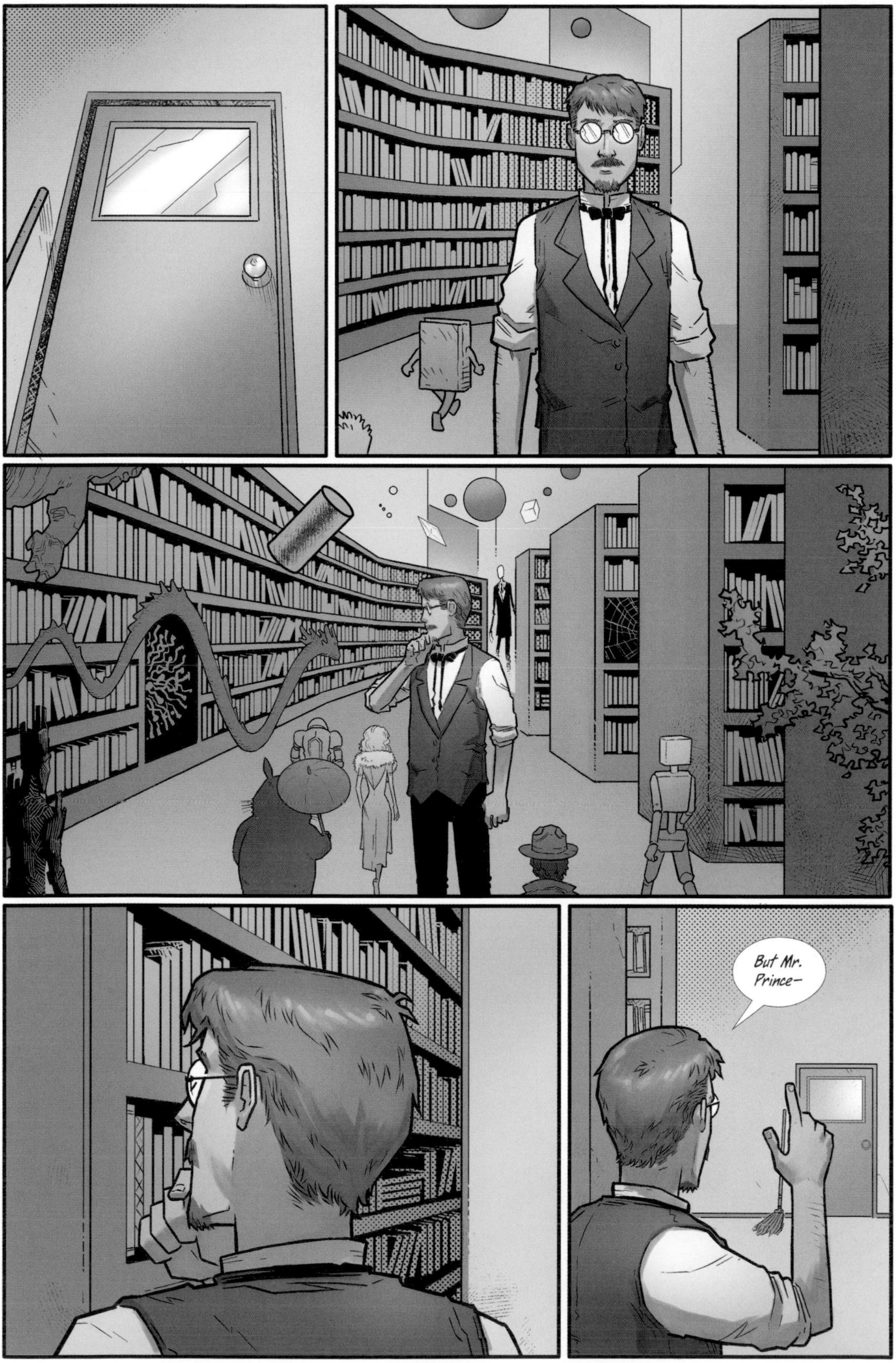
But Mr. Prince–

The End,
I guess.